T0277081

Memories of London

Memories of London

Edmondo De Amicis

Translated by Stephen Parkin

FOLLOWED BY

An Excursion to the Poor Districts of London

Louis Laurent Simonin

Translated by Adam Elgar

ALMA CLASSICS

ALMA CLASSICS LTD

London House
243-253 Lower Mortlake Road
Richmond
Surrey TW9 2LL
United Kingdom
www.almaclassics.com

Memories of London first published in Italian in 1873
An Excursion to the Poor Districts of London first published in French in 1862
These translations first published by Alma Books Ltd in 2014

Translation of *Memories of London* © Stephen Parkin, 2014
Translation of *An Excursion to the Poor Districts of London* © Adam Elgar, 2014

Printed in Great Britain by by CPI Group (UK) Ltd, Croydon, CR0 4YY

ISBN: 978-1-84749-326-2

Contents

Introduction

The writer Edmondo De Amicis, still only in his late twenties, visited London for the first and only time in 1873, just over a decade after the unification of his native country Italy, in the cause of which he had fought as a soldier (and only two years after the completion of that process with the transfer of Rome as its capital to the new nation). He was at the outset of a literary career which was to bring him great fame and popularity with the reading public in Italy and beyond. He became one of the most representative figures of the new publishing industry and readership which emerged in Italy in the years after national unification (a status which was characteristically followed by a proportionate reversal in his critical fortunes after his death in 1908), a professional writer who began his career as a journalist for the Florentine newspaper *La Nazione* and in the course of it turned his hand to various genres, often showing great inventive flair. After publishing his first book, a collection of military sketches based on his experiences as a soldier, which had previously appeared in newspapers, he became a kind of foreign correspondent, sending back reports on his travels to Spain, Morocco, Constantinople, Holland, Paris and London for newspapers and illustrated magazines. Many of these articles formed the basis for subsequent books which capitalized on their initial success in the periodical press. Although De Amicis more or less gave up travel writing a decade or so later – after producing the classic children's book *Cuore* which made him a household name – the genre, with its mixture of objective reportage and subjective impression, its mobility of focus, was a perfect vehicle for his talents as a young writer, notably his descriptive powers and linguistic agility, which critics at the time singled out as his most remarkable gift. It also suited his restless temperament and at times almost febrile curiosity about places and people.

Though much shorter than most of his other travel books, *Memories of London* is a characteristic example of De Amicis's travel writing. First published in 1873 in four parts in the magazine *Nuova Illustrazione Universale*, one of the high-circulation illustrated weekly magazines popular in many European countries of the time, De Amicis was persuaded to reprint them as a book (although he insisted that the publisher Treves added a foreword making it clear they were intended as newspaper articles and had not been revised). Treves decided to add a series of articles, translated into Italian, by the French geologist and radical journalist Louis Laurent Simonin, well known in Italy, on a visit he had made to the poor districts of London, which had appeared in an equivalent French illustrated periodical *Le Tour du Monde* ten years earlier, both in order to make the book rather more substantial and, perhaps as importantly, as Treves himself says, to introduce a telling contrast between two views of the British metropolis: the Italian's impressionistic sketches as he visits the principal sights and the Frenchman's quasi-sociological observation of its grimmer realities.

De Amicis too, as he tells us, had an opportunity to make the same visit as Simonin – in fact he confirms what is clear from the earlier account: that interested visitors to the city could make special arrangements with the police to accompany them on their nightly patrols of the squalid and crime-infested slums of the city's East End – but, perhaps for lack of time, he did not undertake it himself. Instead he goes the round of what was already by the 1870s a well-known and well-worn tourist circuit, including its historical monuments (such as the Tower of London and Westminster Abbey) and its newer marvels of engineering prowess and cultural display (such as Marc Isambard Brunel's celebrated tunnel under the Thames connecting Rotherhithe and Wapping, which had been constructed thirty years earlier, and the renowned architectural feat of Joseph Paxton's Crystal Palace in the suburbs south of the city, built for the Great Exhibition of 1851 and at the time of De Amicis's visit still a major visitor attraction, with its galleries crammed with arts and crafts, objects and animals from around the world, especially the flourishing British Empire). These visits provide the book's set pieces, where De Amicis exploits all his considerable rhetorical abilities to create an effect, but in between these scenes, as in all of his travel writing, there are more informal and seemingly unstructured passages where De Amicis strolls the streets (it is significant, as he tells us, that he prefers to walk round the cities he visits), jotting down random impressions and reflections and anecdotes concerning the buildings and traffic, the appearance of passers-by, odd encounters and snatches of conversation, the shifting effects of light and weather and his own changeable spirits.

Yet De Amicis's record of his visit to London in 1873 is more than just a lively personal account of his experiences: there is a wider underlying resonance, linked to its historical context, which deepens its fascination for readers today, and of which De Amicis himself was certainly aware – the confrontation of a young Italian from a newly established nation with a unique example of a modern-day megalopolis. He explicitly relishes the contrast between London, "a *mare magnum*, a veritable Babylon, a chaos... the largest city on earth", and himself, "on my own... not knowing a word of English [at the time French would have been the second language of educated Italians like De Amicis]... short of money..." The contrast between the solitary visitor and the "vast ocean" of the British capital is also the contrast between mid-nineteenth-century Italy – still comparatively unindustrialized and predominantly agricultural, a dense network of ancient urban centres of which only a handful exceeded a population of 200,000 – and a metropolis which was the hub of world trade and in constant expansion. The philosopher and critic Benedetto Croce commented disdainfully on De Amicis's tiresome tendency to exaggerate in his travel writing, but his amazement at the scale of London in direct comparison with the realities he was familiar with back in his homeland (at one point he asserts that the populations of Greenwich or Chelsea are equivalent to those of Florence or Rome) is genuine and sincere. And it is not just the scale of the city which was remarkable for an Italian: the sheer organization of urban spaces and of the daily flux of work and leisure within them also had no close parallels in the much more traditionally arranged and close-knit cities and towns of Italy. It is not just the extraordinary mass of traffic clogging the streets in the morning rush hour which occasions De Amicis's awe: his wonder at the extent and efficiencies of London's transport network (the double-decker buses, the underground trains, the elevated railway lines winding among the chimney pots, the railway bridges as wide as piazzas), as well as at the continual presence of street signs and directions, making it hard ever to get seriously lost despite the immensity of the place, is also palpable.

De Amicis's later writings – the aforementioned *Cuore* is the outstanding example – reveal a consistent programmatic, pedagogic impulse, usually, but not always, kept subordinate to artistic priorities. Similarly, behind the animated entertaining surface of the account of his visit to the great Victorian capital city in *Memories of London* there is – as with his other travel books – an implicit intention both to broaden Italy's horizons, now that it was itself a nation on the world stage, and also to use those horizons to measure Italians' awareness of their own reality.

– Stephen Parkin

Memories of London

Edmondo De Amicis

I

I T WAS RAINING, the sea was rough, the ship rocked up and down like a small boat. Barely half an hour out from the port of Dieppe I experienced, for the first time in my life, the symptoms of seasickness. There were numerous women on board, most of them English, all cheerfully munching bread and cheese without the slightest sign of even noticing the violent rise and fall of the ship, which set my innards – and those of others, who were already emitting more than just moans – in turmoil. So it's true that seasickness makes a man rise above all worldly vanity! If half an hour earlier someone had said to me: "I'll tell you what – here's enough money to stay in London for a whole month instead of just the fortnight you're going to spend there; enough too for a trip round Scotland, and even over to Ireland. All this money is yours if you're prepared to make a complete fool of yourself in front of these ladies" – I freely confess I'd have been too vain to accept. Now, half an hour later, here I was, utterly despising myself, stretched out on two dirty sacks, one foot pointing east and the other west, my top hat askew over one ear, one trouser leg rolled up showing a stretch of tar-bespattered long johns, and my head lolling to one side with such an air of abandon I could have been a model for a bad statue depicting "Languor". As Fucini* said, you never feel so sick as when you're seasick. To add to my torment, there was some fool of a Frenchman sitting next to me – we'd left Paris together – who kept on saying each time I groaned: "*Mais vous n'êtes pas malade...*"* – pointing to a lady I couldn't even bring myself to look at while all the bystanders laughed. The fair sex! Love! If the most beautiful creature on earth had said to me, like Hugo's Duchess Josiane to the clown Gwynplaine, "I love you, I accept you, come to my arms!"* I wouldn't even have turned my head to look at her. Even the thought which had so excited me that morning – "This evening I'll be in London!" – now just made me feel even more wretched. In my delirious ramblings I thought to myself, "And to think I chose to come to London for the sake of amusement. Madman! And to think I'll have to cross the sea to get back again! No, no, it's impossible: I'd rather die! I'll stay in England, I'll find a job, I'll become a shop assistant, teach Italian, anything so long as I never set eyes on the sea again. When my time's up, I'll die quietly, but I never want to have to face this torture ever again!

A few hours later I was dining in the restaurant in Brighton station, the idea of ending my days in England now abandoned.

It was getting dark when I caught the train to London. I snuggled into the corner seat of my compartment and started to turn over in my mind the extraordinary thought that in a few hours' time I would be in London. London! I kept repeating, enjoying the sound of the word, just as you enjoy the sound of a gold coin spinning on a tabletop. London! I took pleasure in the thought – as if it were the first time it had occurred to me – that London is unbelievably vast, a *mare magnum*, a veritable Babylon, a chaos, something quite unreal. It's the largest city on earth, I thought – and that's a kind of absolute no other city can achieve, since, while there might be more beautiful cities, with these one can never be certain which one in particular is the most beautiful; whereas the thought that London's size makes it incontestably supreme is strangely pleasurable. It's impossible to hold the thought in your mind without entering the realm of dreams, the idea of something of which you can say, "No one has ever seen anything larger!" And the thought I was going to London on my own – not knowing anyone there, carrying no letters of introduction – cheered me: it was the best state to be in to experience getting lost on that vast ocean, with that feeling amounting almost to fear which vast untracked spaces can arouse, to feel overwhelmed, to receive, in a word, as fully and as clearly as possible the impression the vastness of London can make on the mind of a foreign visitor. And, what is more, I also had the advantage of not knowing a word of English, of being short of money and carrying a small and pitifully shabby-looking case – all that's needed, in short, to feel as tiny and pathetic as possible in a huge foreign metropolis. As I turned these thoughts over and over in my mind, I rubbed my hands and declared, "London, I'm ready for you!"

Night had fallen when I reached the city. We entered it without my noticing, and I was surprised when I was told it was time to get off the train. I descended from the carriage and found myself under the vast roof of London Bridge station, surrounded by a chaos of carriages and lights. I got into the nearest hansom cab and showed the driver a piece of paper with written on it the name of the hotel which others had recommended to me in Paris and the street on which it was located. The cab driver read it, nodded to show he'd understood, and didn't move. I gestured towards the box for him to get up onto it and leave. Not a twitch. I started to swear at him in French, of which he didn't understand a word; calmly leaning against the door of the cab he started a long speech in English. "Now I'm done for!" I said to myself. "What do I do now?" I crossed my arms and stared at him. He crossed his arms and stared back. So we stared at each other for a few moments. Finally I lost patience, climbed down from the cab and, shouting "You donkey!" straight into his face, went on my way by myself. I realized afterwards he hadn't wanted to take me to my hotel because the distance was too great. By myself! But what was I to do? And where was I to go? I confess I suddenly felt discouraged. The vast station from which I couldn't find the way out, the fact I didn't know which direction to follow, that unfortunate first encounter with the cabman which seemed like a bad omen, the heavy case I had to drag along, the damp air seeping into me, the night, the confusion – I suddenly felt miserable and full of dismay. After wandering aimlessly round for a while, I finally went through a door and found myself outside the station. It was like being plunged into chaos. The endless rattling of carriages I couldn't see, the whistle of trains coming from I knew not where, lights above and below and all around, a thick fog which meant I couldn't distinguish shapes or judge distances, and crowds of people rushing to and fro as if they were running away from something: this was the first spectacle of the city. Wobbling and limping, I made my way along the street, dazed, hardly able to think; then, my case being too heavy to carry any more, I set it down and stopped. As luck would have it, when I raised my eyes I saw a coloured sign with the words *On parle français* on it. It was a hotel. I drew a sigh of relief, picked up my burden and entered with the air of the country mouse coming to town for the first time. A bad-tempered woman – the owner – called a waiter over as soon as I began to speak. I asked him if they had a room. The waiter – spitting forth every word of French as if he were retching and looking me up and down with that air of solicitude and disdain typical of his trade – replied that yes, they had a room available, but... but – he added – it cost five shillings. And he gave me another suspicious look. It's perfectly true that my clothes justified his misgivings. Nevertheless, with all the scorn of a born millionaire, I threw a sovereign onto the counter and, with a gesture which could have accompanied a line of Dante, proclaimed, "Take your money and show me to my room!" They took me to the room. I threw myself immediately on the bed, but for a long time I couldn't keep my eyes closed, such was the assault on my ears. It was a dull monotonous noise, as if the waves of the sea were crashing against the ground floor of the hotel, and in the midst of this murmur sharp sounds exploded as if from afar, filling my head with strange images, as though they were words which escaped the immense metropolis while it was sleeping: groans from its endless suburbs, curses from the extraordinary careworn City, accusations and pleas, like the roar of a stormy sea. Gradually the louder noises died away, leaving only the monotonous murmur; every now and then, the loud noises would begin again – it takes time for a city like London to become drowsy – and then again ceased; and finally I fell asleep and had the most extraordinary dreams.

In the morning, well before sunrise, I left the hotel and headed towards the Thames. I was very near London Bridge, in the heart of the City. There was almost no one about and not a sound to be heard; the sky was grey and it was cold; a light mist covered everything, but not so much you couldn't make things out. I walked briskly towards the bridge, since I knew the most remarkable view of London could be had from there.

When I got to the middle of the bridge I looked around. A sudden chill ran through me from the top of my head to the soles of my feet, and I stood stock still. The image of Paris seen from the Pont Neuf floated into my mind: it now seemed unbelievably small. I leant on the parapet and, with the air of someone trying to put some order into his thoughts, said to myself: "Now, let's see what we've got here."

Beneath me, the broad stretch of the Thames: on one side ships lined up as far as the eye could see, on the other a series of huge bridges; along either riverbank, near to London Bridge, massy black houses, like ancient fortresses, in a disordered line directly on the water's edge. A bit farther along, large, sinister-looking buildings with vast vaulted roofs like those of railway stations; and beyond these, the broken and only vaguely visible outlines of edifices gradually greying in the distance, until all that could be made out was a vast and misty confusion of chimney stacks, towers, domes and steeples; and farther still, shadowy views of what almost seemed to be other distant cities, more imagined than seen, forming a slight wavy line on the grey horizon. On all the nearby buildings, bridges and riverbanks, a dark factory-like griminess hung, a worn-out air of effort and weariness, clammy and gloomy, like the bleakness of city streets after a fire has swept through them – it was an immense and melancholy sight.

But the mind plays such strange tricks! Just when we are beholding a spectacle which should be enough to absorb our attention entirely, at least for the first time, our thoughts suddenly dart a thousand miles off to think of something completely unconnected with the scene before us and so trivial we'd scorn to think twice about it in the ordinary run of things. I was seeing London for the first time, but I was thinking about a volume of Voltaire's works I had lent and had not had returned to me before leaving Turin.

Then I forgot about the book and, as always happens when you find yourself in an unknown city, a thousand different images of the people and things I used to imagine seeing in the place before my arrival flocked into my head, like the background in a painting: beer-bellied shopkeepers out of the pages of Dickens, Queen Elizabeth, an English family I'd spotted on one occasion in Florence admiring Ghiberti's baptistery doors,* the gesture my father made once saying how much he would give to see London, and the portrait of the actor Garrick* I'd seen in an illustrated magazine.

And then another unexplained thought distracted me: I realized I hadn't shaved and asked myself where I was going to eat breakfast.

And then again a sudden wonder at finding myself there, as if I'd fallen out of the sky, overcame me, which in turn disappeared after about a minute, to be replaced by an icy indifference, as if I'd always been there – and then the sense of marvel flooded back again, just like before. St Augustine was right: travel seems almost pointless if we compare the extraordinary goings-on in our heads with all the things we see around us!

I crossed the bridge and entered the small square on the left bank, and then took one of the streets, all of them empty, which lead towards St Paul's Cathedral. I turned right and found myself after a few more paces in the fish market, in a narrow street, wet and dark, so packed with carts and people it was difficult to move. I walked on, immersed in such a strong smell of herrings that after a minute or so I could have wiped a piece of bread on my clothes and breakfasted off that, and reached the famous Tower of London, the city's Bastille. I circled it, gazing with trepidation on its sinister walls, and went on hurriedly into the docks, intending to take a circular route so I wouldn't have to retrace my steps. The streets were long and winding, with high dark walls on either side, like prison walls, windowless and doorless; hundreds of workmen stood unmoving at the street corners while other groups disappeared silently down dark alleyways. For half an hour I saw nothing else, just walking along those monotonous streets like the winding passageways inside an ancient fortress, feeling bored and melancholy, without the slightest idea where I would emerge. At a certain point, after a long while, I realized I was returning along the route I had taken, so I had to go on a new and lengthy detour to get back in the proper direction. I'd left St Katherine Docks behind me and, thinking I'd reached the end of the London Docks, decided to walk as far as the India Docks. I turned into a street I couldn't see the end of; on the right there were the dock walls and on the left small houses, in the midst of which other long, narrow streets stretched away between factory towers, warehouse walls, smoke-blackened houses all jumbled together. As I strode on, it seemed to me that, far from getting farther and farther out of London, I was approaching the centre. But I was unconcerned and went on walking – I trusted my legs would hold out and, after all, I'd never needed a carriage in Paris, much to the amazement of my friends, as I'd always preferred to walk. However, after a while it occurred to me that it might be useful to know exactly where I was. Passing by a group of workmen, I heard French being spoken, so I stopped and asked one of them if the building in front of me was the India Dock.

All I got in reply was my question repeated – "Is that the India Dock?" – and a look as though I were out of my mind.

"Well, is it or isn't it?"

With a laugh the answer came: "I can see, sir, you're not familiar with London! This is the London Dock."

"I'm still in the London Dock! But I've been walking for half an hour since I entered the main gate."

"And so? Don't you know that the area of the London Dock just for tobacco goes on for more than a mile?"

"So how much farther is it to the India Docks?"

"By train or by boat?"

"On foot!"

He looked at my feet.

"I wouldn't really know…" he replied. "Maybe four or five miles."

"And what's there to see in these four or five miles?"

"Houses, docks, warehouses, factories, industrial plants…"

"All the time?"

"All the time."

"And what comes after the India Docks?"

"The Outer Dock."

"And how far is that from the India Docks?"

"About another five miles."

"Five miles of houses and factories?"

"That's right – houses and factories."

"And after the Outer Dock?"

"You go as far as Greenwich on the other side of the river."

"How far is that?"

"Two or three miles."

"All built up?"

"All built up."

"And after Greenwich?"

"After Greenwich there's the East India Import Dock."

"How far is that from Greenwich?"

"About eight miles."

"Houses and factories?"

"Houses and factories."

"And after that?"

"After that it goes on."

"And where does it end?"

"God only knows!"

Now it was my turn to look at my feet. I took my leave of the workman and, crestfallen, retraced my steps as I said to myself, "You poor fool! You thought you could come to London and walk from one end of the city to the other just like that!"

I went back through the fish market, past London Bridge again, and set off in the direction of the city centre.

When I reached Fleet Street, the rush hour was in full swing.

Finally, I saw London.

B OTH PAVEMENTS WERE PACKED with people, as if
they had just emerged from a theatre, but there were
no knots or groups of people or anyone shouting and gestur-
ing; each person hurried along in silence, taking advantage
of every little gap which opened up to move ahead of the
pedestrian in front. People bumped into each other but didn't
turn round. In the middle of the road a long line of large
omnibuses went by. They were brightly painted, like carni-
val floats, with a kind of winding staircase in front which
widens as it ascends and holds the passengers fanned out;
lower down they're almost touching the ground, while above
they're on a level with the first floor of the buildings and can
lean over the sides, as though they were floating in mid-air. In
between the omnibuses and on either side of them there was
an indescribable confusion of horse carts, carriages, hansom
cabs, drays, caleches, barrows and wagons covered with
advertising, moving contraptions of every shape and size,
three, five, even eight abreast, the horses pulling them with

their muzzles touching the behinds of the horses in front, the wheel hubs glancing off each other, endless manoeuvrings as they twisted in and out, with intricate groups of dozens of vehicles first forming and then, with difficulty, disentangling, so that at any moment you thought the whole creaking mass of them would suddenly fall to pieces like a large machine breaking up under a hammer blow. Heavily laden porters, boys pushing handcarts, men carrying publicity sandwich boards ran between the vehicles and along the pavements as though fleeing for their lives. At every street corner this huge torrent of people and things flows off in broad canals and is replenished with tributary crowds, expands and stagnates in squares and courtyards, filters into rills which twist through the narrow alleys and passageways among the houses. As I was borne along the current I suddenly heard a high-pitched whistle above my head. I raised my eyes and saw a steam train passing over a high bridge which spanned the street. No sooner had this train gone by than I heard another whistle on the other side and turned round to see another train passing over the chimney tops of the houses along the road. And at the same moment, coming from the opposite direction, a cloud of smoke issued forth from a large opening in the ground: it was a third train, this time on the underground network, which, upon seeing the daylight as it passed through a sudden gap in the tunnel, sounded its whistle in greeting. I reached the corner of a broad street leading down to the Thames. I could see the river and its bridges: moving across the bridges in both directions there were yet more trains, while passing under the arches steamboats lowered their funnels like great trees bowed by the wind and tugboats pulled long rows of barges; on the river there were swarms of little boats and rafts, while across the bridges long processions of people passed, disappearing on the other side. As I walked on I saw more seemingly endless streets between enormous buildings, all filled with crowds. And all around me a cacophony – the iron bridges groaning under the weight of the long trains sounding their whistles and breathlessly whooshing out steam, above and below me, near and far, on the ground, in the air, along the water; a furious race of departures and arrivals, continuous meetings, escapes, pursuits, accompanied by the sound of cracks and squeaks and thuds and bangs; the confusion of a vast battlefield together with the clockwork order of an immense factory; and then the darkness of the sky, the gloomy buildings, the silent crowds and their serious faces – all this gave an air of mystery and pain to the spectacle, as if all that huge motion were the product of ineluctable necessity and all that endless labour a form of damnation. Dazed and exhausted I took refuge inside a pub and heaved a long sigh: "What kind of world is this? How can people live in this way?"

After a while I set out again and walked as far as Trafalgar Square, right in the centre of the area most frequented by foreigners. I liked the tall column rising up in the fog with the noble Lord Nelson standing on top of it, and I admired the four great lions which encircle its base, but the square itself didn't match up to my expectations, perhaps because I compared it with the Place de la Concorde in Paris. It's the terminus for all the omnibuses serving the western part of the city, so you can just imagine the confusion which reigns. I laughed at the thought that what we call a great crowd in Via del Corso in Rome or Via Toledo in Naples or certain main streets in Genoa seems like a village fête compared to what you see in Trafalgar Square. From here I walked down Whitehall as far as Parliament Square, and then went on to Westminster Bridge.

The view from the bridge is the most beautiful in London, surpassing all the views from the bridges along the Seine.

On one side there is the huge, delicate Gothic edifice of the Houses of Parliament, crowned with innumerable turrets and adorned with a thousand statues of kings and queens. Behind it rise the towers of the glorious Abbey of Westminster, England's Pantheon, while on the opposite bank of the river there are the eight elegant and brightly painted buildings of St James's Hospital.* When you look upriver a wide, cheerful horizon opens out before you; it's as if you're in another city, a southern one, serene and majestic. This stretch of the Thames has only a few steamers and boats on it; the river flows silently in front of the Parliament building, symbol of England's power and glory, like a vast army parading before its king. From those quiet, clear spaces you look back and see far off, as though through a veil, the jumble of blackened buildings, the bridges swarming with pedestrians, the dark smoky city fretting and labouring.

While I was standing on Westminster Bridge, I noticed for the first time that in London, whenever the streets become busy, many men – including gentlemen – roll their trouser legs up like peasants. Many of them also wear gaudy poseys of flowers in their buttonholes. I confess I had to laugh whenever I saw – as I often did – a man with a very serious

View of Westminster Palace from the south bank of the Thames

expression on his face but sporting one of these poseys and wearing his trouser legs rolled up.

I walked back across the bridge and explored the main streets. The map I'd brought with me was useful, and I didn't need to ask anyone for directions.

It's hard to describe what the streets of London look like. No other city presents such a disorderly variety of forms, such an extraordinary mixture of the beautiful and the ugly, the splendid and the squalid, of bleakness, eccentricity, grandeur and dullness. Taken all together it seems like a city you're unfamiliar with but which is made up of many other cities you've already visited, all given a uniformity to conceal their different origins. The different architectural styles of every other country and every other historical period have been gathered together, combined and superimposed. Walking down just one street you come across Arab, Byzantine, Gothic and classical as well as the various native styles of building; a single edifice might have pointed arches and a Greek peristyle, Moorish columns and Renaissance caryatids, a roof in the style of an Indian pagoda and walls like those of an Egyptian temple. At every street corner you see something which transports you a thousand miles away – some garbled memory of Venice, a vague hint of Rome, a sudden glimpse of Seville or Cologne, and, a bit farther on, a stretch of street like something in Paris. All these features which have been seen elsewhere are blackened by London's soot and smog and seem more austere, as if saddened at being so far away from their native land or upset at finding themselves surrounded by the foggy air, the noise, the sight of the city's fretful existence. What is more, all this over-abundance of columns and pediments and turrets and swags and reliefs and ornaments and monumental shapes has an ostentatious, weary air about it. All that art seems imported and ill at ease in its new surroundings. There's an excess, a profligacy of riches and luxury for the sake of appearances. The city has bought its beauty and is like a merchant's wife dressed up and made over.

In contrast to the streets lined with princely mansions, there are others, very long, consisting of endless rows of identical houses – the same colour, the same height, the same shape – with their roofs hidden behind their façades in such a way they appear to be roofless; the façades are as bare as ramparts, with no balconies or shutters, and the doors and windows have thin white borders which give them the look of giant catafalques, or, elsewhere, are dark red or a dirty-looking yellow, so they seem made out of mud or soot. You can walk for miles down streets lined with houses with walls and colours like this without coming across a single building which breaks their bleak monotony, a single house which recalls the city of wealth and splendour.

But the wealth and splendour of the well-off neighbourhoods are in turn an amazing contrast. With every step you take there's an edifice dripping with sculptural reliefs and ornamental features which at first sight you think must be a royal palace but turns out to be a railway station, a hotel or an emporium. There are whole streets lined on both sides with these splendid giants: if you stand at the farthest corner of one of them, the others seem to be miles away, their black shapes looming through the fog like the sheer sides of cliffs. The grandeur of other cities is dispersed, and you need to seek it out, but here it surrounds you – and what seems grand in other cities, if you imagine it in the context of London, shrinks and vanishes. You walk across a neighbourhood full of monuments, you pass from a city of mansions, as quiet as if it were uninhabited, to one of factories, full of a thousand different noises, where you see no one around, and then to a suburb packed full of people but silent as a tomb, and then back again into a city of mansions. You're not walking around a city: you're travelling through an entire country.

Who could possibly recount the thousands of fleeting impressions which come to you as you stroll by yourself round a city like London? You keep marvelling at intervals, but also between each moment of marvel you feel nothing more than tedium and fatigue. Every five minutes you ask yourself, "But am I really enjoying myself? Is this all that the pleasure of travel amounts to?" Sometimes a fear overcomes you that you'll collapse in the middle of the street and that you'll end up touched by who knows whom and carried off who knows where. Other spots invite mysterious analogies with other places and people and circumstances, so that you think you've been here before, some time in the past, at exactly the same time, with the sunlight falling in precisely that fashion, and with the same smell in the air. On occasion an inexplicable cheerfulness takes hold of you: you're seized with a sudden love of the place and regard the passers-by with a benevolent eye, as if they were all your friends. At other times a stranger's unfriendly glance or rude answer makes you so dispirited that you hate the place and see nothing good in it. The sad whining sound of a street organ in certain dark and crowded streets evokes confusedly in your head the countless mysterious sufferings and crimes lurking in those vast human anthills; you long to be elsewhere, in the fresh air, in a country villa you once glimpsed from the window of a carriage ten years before.

Once, at a particular time of day, I found myself near to a station of the underground railway and decided to take a trip on it. I went down two or three staircases to find myself all of a sudden transported from broad daylight to the middle of night: flickering lights, people, noise, trains arriving and disappearing out of and into the dark. My train comes in and stops; its passengers hurry out and those waiting jump into the carriages. As I try to work out where the second-class compartments are, the train leaves. "What's happening? Doesn't it stop?!" I asked one of the station staff. "Don't you worry, sir, here's another one coming in." The trains don't just arrive one after the other, they seem to be pursuing each other. It comes in, I jump aboard, and off it moves, as swift as an arrow. A new spectacle begins. We run between the foundations of the city, deep in the unknown. First we descend into an impenetrable darkness, followed by a brief glimpse of feeble daylight; then back into the dark, interrupted every now and then by strange flashes of light; then we emerge into a station lit by hundreds of lamps, only for the station to disappear after a moment. Other trains pass by, but you can't see them. There's a sudden stop at a station, with the thousand faces of the waiting crowd lit up as if by a great fire; and then off we go again, with a deafening noise of doors being slammed shut, bells being rung, machinery grunting; again darkness, more trains passing by, more glimpses of daylight, more illuminated stations, more crowds of people passing, arriving, leaving, until we reach the terminus. I hurry out, the train disappears, I'm pushed through a doorway and half carried up a staircase until I re-emerge into the light of day. But where am I? What city am I in? How will I find my way from here? Calmly does it – let's go into a pub and have a look at the map.

After a long examination of the map, I work out how to get to the British Museum, which, of all the museums in London, is the one I'm most curious to see. I hurry through the vast halls of sculpture, of Egyptian and Assyrian antiquities, and stop in the Manuscripts Room to look at a tenancy agreement signed by Shakespeare and a sales contract for *Paradise Lost*, and innumerable other autographs of the

Underground station

St Paul's Cathedral

world's greatest artists and rulers. But out of all these only two made such a profound impression on me that I couldn't take my eyes off them for a while. They're two small scraps of paper. On one of them there's a sum and on the other a few small circles, some drawn along a straight line in the middle and some crowded into a corner of the sheet; both the sum and the circles appear to have been drawn in haste by an unsteady hand. Out of all the manuscripts in the Museum, these two sheets of paper must have been written and drawn on the most solemn of occasions. Who can even begin to imagine what was in the minds of the two men as they jotted down those numbers and circles, the storm which raged in their souls! The numbers represent the mustered forces of the English army and were written on the eve of the Battle of Waterloo; the circles represent the ships of the English and French fleets shortly before the Battle of Abukir.* The numbers were jotted down by Wellington; the circles were drawn by Nelson. There are manuscripts by Galileo, Newton, Michelangelo, Franklin, Washington, Molière, Charles V, Peter the Great, Dürer, Luther, Tasso, Rousseau, Cromwell... enough and to spare. But here's another strange thing: now I don't know what I wouldn't give to see even one of those manuscripts, but at the time, when all I had to do was bend over the display cases to look at them, I didn't feel even a flicker of curiosity. And what is even stranger is that even then I knew I would later regret not having looked at them. I scolded myself: "But aren't you interested to see them?" To which I replied, "I've no idea." I just felt a wretched desire to leave, and ran through the rooms of the museum with barbaric indifference to the many treasures in the midst of which one could spend a whole month of continual enjoyment.

"*Mi paghi, no!*"*

As I was leaving the museum, I heard a stranger just about to go in grumble these words. "Oh my sweet mother tongue!" I said to myself, and stopped to take a look at the man. He had the appearance of a labourer and was talking to a woman who seemed to be his wife. He noticed that I had turned to look at them and turned round himself, but when he saw me smiling this led to a series of misunderstandings. Instead of realizing I was his fellow countryman adrift on the vast ocean of the city – that his words "*mi paghi, no*" had warmed my heart and that, if I'd dared to, I would have taken the greatest pleasure in inviting them both to dine with me – what enters his head? The thought that I'm making eyes at his wife. My kindly expression is met by a hostile gaze and, seeing that I go on looking at them, he steps forward as if he's going to punch me on the nose! "Ungrateful Lombard that you are!" I murmured sadly as I went on my way. What a blow to the heart you've given me! But let it be, I forgive you, for the sake for our motherland!

Before evening fell, I wanted to take a trip on the elevated railway line, so I bought a return ticket for a station chosen at random. The pleasure of travelling on this railway is completely different from that felt on the underground, but equally vivid. You roll along up among the roofs, in the region of smoke and swallows, across an endless forest of chimney pots, pipes, weather vanes and garret windows; you glimpse thousands of little tucked-away features of that capricious, inchoate, solitary architecture, which, like some wild hanging garden, covers the top floor of the city's buildings; you see into thousands of small windows, little dens of humanity, houses suspended like cages between the sky and earth, yet with large families nesting in them, tending little aerial terrace gardens; and when you lift your eyes you can see far off into the surrounding distance, with an occasional glimpse of the Thames, the masts of the ships in the port, the green spaces of large parks, factory towers in the suburbs, everything except where this extraordinary panorama ends.

I still had to finish the last part of my journey by bus. I climbed onto the upper deck of the first one I saw, travelled as far as the final stop and then stayed on it to return to where I'd started. As the bus went along, I was frequently astonished by the casual familiarity shown by my fellow passengers, who, as they moved along to take their seats, used my shoulder to lean on, letting me feel their whole weight, and then gave me a hearty blow as they lifted their hands, like an athlete pushing the pole away after he's vaulted the rope. The first passenger to do me this kindness so took me by surprise I was left speechless. I turned round expecting to see the perpetrator give me a smile as if to say "Sorry!" Not a bit of it! He turned his back on me without so much as giving me a glance. Now that I'd grasped that this was the way things were done, I took due precautions and, every time I saw a passenger stretch out his hand, I turned my shoulder in his direction with a "Feel free" and, holding firm until he'd let it go, managed to feel a bit less crushed. But on the same bus journey I was also compensated by the pleasure I took in convincing myself that it is perfectly possible for two people to have an enjoyable conversation without understanding a word of what the other one is saying. A young man with a very cheerful air was sitting next to me and spoke to me in English. I replied in French, "I don't understand." He didn't understand I hadn't understood and went on talking and laughing. I shook my head as if to say no, no, please don't bother yourself, you're wasting your breath. But as chance seemed to have it, the "no" appeared to be the right answer to a question he had just asked me, so he continued to talk even more enthusiastically. So, seeing that he took such pleasure in speaking to me, I pretended to understand, with half-smiles and vague nods which couldn't contradict outright anything he was saying to me. But I grew bored with this and, deciding that if he was speaking a language I didn't understand I might just as well speak to him in a language he would find incomprehensible, started to talk in Italian. He was totally in the dark, but nevertheless laughed, slapped my knee and listened to me with curiosity, as though I'd sung him a song. Then he started off again in English, and so we went on for quite a while, to our mutual satisfaction, until the bus stopped. We got off, he handed me a timetable for a steamship company, for which I imagine he was an agent, and we took leave of each other with a handshake, for all the world like two people who'd found themselves in complete agreement on all the burning issues of the day.

In the evening I didn't have the courage to challenge the onset of low spirits and took refuge from them by going back to the hotel early. If only there had been somebody there I could have paid to listen to me, I would willingly have given them a half-sovereign, such was my need to let off steam by talking, after seeing so many things without being able to speak about any of them! So, not knowing what else to do, I set about preparing the comparisons and the images I would need, when I was back home, to give an idea of the size of London; and since for many days past I'd done nothing but browse guidebooks and ask all the people I met for information, I was certainly not short of material.

So let me tell you – I said, addressing the armchair chosen to stand in for a close friend – that London is sixteen miles across and covers an area of thirty-five square miles; that the towns which are gradually becoming part of it are equivalent to the population of Florence, in the case of Greenwich, or Rome, in the case of Chelsea, or Marseille, in the case of Hackney; that the number of domestic servants alone in the city is greater than the whole of the Italian army in peacetime; that the gas lamps which illuminate its ten thousand streets would light a street a quarter of the length of the earth's circumference; that, based on the estimate that it takes ten litres of beer to get a German drunk, the amount of beer consumed in a single year in London would make the entire German army, under wartime conscription, drunk twice over; that if all the cows, sheep and pigs which are eaten in a single year in London were put in a line they would stretch across the continent of Europe, from the Straits of Gibraltar to the northernmost tip of Russia; that all the oysters swallowed in London over twelve months would cover the entire Champ de Mars, together with the Pont d'Iena and the Place du Trocadero, in Paris; and that London Bridge is crossed each and every day by twenty thousand carriages.

On the following morning I went off to visit the Crystal Palace.

3

THE SHORT TRIP from Victoria station to the Crystal
Palace offers as much variety as a long journey. First,
in the midst of other fast-moving trains you cross over a
wide bridge, as big as a town square, suspended over the
Thames, on which the rails interlink so densely the surface
seems entirely made of iron. You pass next to the large
park in Battersea, followed by stations, tunnels, factories
surrounded by hundreds of workers' houses, like little villages within the city, all the houses identical in shape and
colour, each with a little garden attached and swarms of
children everywhere. Then come further parks, the outlines
of huge buildings under construction, warehouses, gardens,
castles, cemeteries and, as far as the eye can see, great
heaps of building material from which new cities will arise
in the future. Under the tunnels, on roof beams, even on
chimney stacks, or trees, or the edges of roads, there's an
extraordinary profusion of boastful advertisements, which
overlay each other like the competing cries of hawkers at a

market and give the whole place the fantastic appearance of one vast bazaar.

At last you see the enormous bulk of the Crystal Palace on top of a hill, displaying the delicate majesty of its transparent vaults to the entire county of Kent.

The interior is formed of one immense hall, like a small world. On first entering, you're completely disoriented. You go from a courtyard into a café, from a café into a bazaar, from a bazaar into a garden, from a garden into a museum. In the midst of cypresses, laurels, aloes and palms and other luxuriant tropical trees, you can see giraffes' necks stretching up or spot the heads of statues by Michelangelo. In the distance, between the sphinxes guarding an Egyptian courtyard, you can make out a Greek house with the Laocoon and the Venus de Milo; from here the gaze wanders off deep into the mysterious chambers of the Alhambra, and from the Alhambra you look out into the courtyard of a small house in Pompeii. You leave the Alhambra, pass through groups of lions and tigers fighting, between two rows of eagles and cockatoos, and emerge into a Byzantine courtyard, from where, through a sequence of doors, you can see the courtyard of a medieval house, a hall in a Renaissance palace, the chapel of a Gothic church. You walk past the monumental tombs, the fountains, the doors painted and carved with images and the masterpieces of modern sculpture, and join a crowd of people waiting at the doors of a theatre to see a performance of *Il trovatore*. A bit farther on, you see on one side an orchestra pit which can hold three thousand musicians under a semi-cupola twice as wide as the dome of St Paul's, and on the other a stage from which a professor is giving a lecture on mathematics. You go past theatres, darkrooms, circuses, you enter the maze of a grand bazaar in the form of temples and pavilions, where the most splendid manufacturing products from all the nations – Cairo to Birmingham, Paris to Peking – are on display. You go down library corridors, through long rows of pianos, carriages, furniture, flower vases, to find yourself lost in the trees and caves of a forest peopled by savages out of Africa or Oceania, roaming as they hunt wild beasts or with their families gathered round the fire, or crouched behind a rock as they take aim at you with their bow and arrows. You go up a staircase: long galleries stretch away into the distance as far as the eye can see. You can walk for miles past oil paintings, watercolours, photographs, the busts of famous men. And above these there are more galleries to wander round, from which, if you look outside, you can see the beautiful county of Kent and, if you look down, the fantastic circuit of rooms and gardens and courtyards and theatres and restaurants, with people going up, going down, crowding into the theatres, disappearing and reappearing among the plants and statues; and over and above all that extraordinary variety of shapes and colours and sights, this compendium of the world under a curving crystal sky, the sun floods in, throws its beams in every direction, casting rainbows, flashes and sparkles of silver along the bluish glass of the walls and vaulting.

On the way back to London something occurred which made me bitterly regret my lack of English. In the carriage there was a gentleman smoking a pipe. I lit the last remaining Virginia cigar from a packet I had carried like a reliquary from Paris. I'd just lit up when a lady came into the compartment. I made a gesture as though to ask her if my smoking bothered her. She said a few words in English which, to judge from the expression on her face, I took to mean "Yes, it does" – so, mustering all my powers of self-sacrifice, I threw the cigar out of the window. No sooner had I done so than the gentleman took hold of my arm and told me in French that the lady had on the contrary replied that she enjoyed the smell of smoke. I looked out the window, empty-handed, while the lady laughed and… *I gasped and felt one moment more were death!**

Once we'd arrived back in London, I went to visit Westminster Abbey, the equivalent of the Church of Santa Croce in Florence.

If you found yourself alone on entering this church you would bow down and kiss the paving stones. It is a Pantheon and, as such, like an argument constructed in marble to prove the immortality of our souls.

On crossing the threshold your eyes immediately look up at the high pointed arches of the roof vaults, before turning to observe the throng of statues surrounding us. The great men of history crowd together, step on one another's toes, hide behind each other. A little way in there is Pitt, Palmerston, Robert Peel – a worthy vanguard for the whole company. There in a corner is Pasquale Paoli.* The more glorious personages depicted there mingle with the less glorious ones but, instead of obscuring them, they cast their radiance on them as well: as a Pantheon it is a divine democracy. The great rulers rest beside the great poets. Alongside Shakespeare there is an educationalist, Andrew Bell;* next to Newton a military standard-bearer; between two victorious admirals the actor Garrick, stepping out from the stage curtains with a smile on his lips. Among a crowd of chamberlains, abbots and ministers, leaving one indifferent, one comes across, like friends met by chance in a foreign country, dear and glorious images which make the heart beat faster: Gray, Milton, Thomson, Thackeray, Addison and the latest arrival, Charles Dickens, loved and lamented as much as the greatest of them. Surrounded by celebrated military captains who shed blood on sea and land, the glory of great benefactors shines out serene and unalloyed: those who fought for the abolition of slavery; the philanthropist Hanway; the physician Wintringham; James Watt, the inventor of the steam engine.* Alongside the dazzling greatness of genius, the austere greatness of upright souls, of indomitable characters, of long lives spent in patient work and unrecognized sacrifice. How many different thoughts arise in those chapels clad in marvellous patterns of stonework, as you walk among the tombs of princes, the memories of the power and the misfortunes of seven royal dynasties! If all the blood which, by the blow of the dagger or the axe, spurted from the veins of the people buried between the tomb of Henry VII and that of Edward the Confessor were to flow again into the sanctuary, not an inch of the marble floor would be left unstained. Mary Stuart, Henry Stafford, the husband of Anna, Duchess of Somerset, beheaded; Thomas Thynne, murdered; Aymer de Valence, 2nd Earl of Pembroke, murdered; Thomas of Woodstock, Duke of Gloucester, murdered; Richard II, murdered; Edward V and his brother the Duke of York, the unhappy sons of Edward IV, both murdered; Spencer Perceval, Chancellor of the Exchequer, assassinated; Nicholas Bagenall, suffocated in his cradle by his nurse. After I had gone round the chapels, I seized the opportunity when the guard was not looking to sit on the ancient throne of the Scottish kings and touch with my hand the stone on which Jacob the patriarch had rested his head and dreamt his visionary dream.*

If you haven't seen London in the rain, you can't really say you have seen the city. I had the pleasure of this experience

44

the morning I went to see the tunnel under the Thames. I could appreciate why you might be tempted to shoot yourself in such weather. The houses dripped water as if they were sweating. It didn't seem as if the water was simply falling from the sky, but as though it was oozing from the stones in the walls and out of the ground. The dark houses get even darker and take on a greasy appearance; the openings to alleyways seem like caves. Everything is dirty, worn, mouldy, sinister; your eyes search in vain for a pleasant sight they can rest on; shivers run through you which seem like a sudden attack of illness; a sense of weariness afflicts you, of disgust with everything, an inexpressible wish to disappear in a flash from this tedious world.

As these thoughts were running through my head, I did indeed disappear from the world, as I descended the steps of an illuminated spiral staircase going down into the earth on the south bank of the Thames opposite the Tower of London. Down and down I went, between two dark walls, until I found myself in front of the circular opening to the gigantic iron tube which floats like some enormous intestine in the innards of the river. Inside the tube there is an underground passageway, the end of which cannot be seen, lit by a long row of lamps which cast a dim light, like the lamps you find on tombs. The air is foggy. You walk for long stretches without meeting a soul. The walls drip like the sides of an aqueduct, and the planking beneath you moves like the deck of a ship. You hear the steps and the voices of people approaching before you actually see them, reverberating as in a cave while, seen from afar, they cast huge shadows. There is in short something mysterious about the place, which, while not exactly frightening, induces a vague sense of anxiety. Then, when you reach halfway and can no longer see where you came in or where you go out, and a grave-like silence descends and you don't know how much farther you have to walk, and you start to think about the depths of the river below you, where the bodies of suicides drift, and about the ships passing over your head and what if a crack opened in the wall and how you wouldn't even have the time to commend your soul to God and... how beautiful the sunlight seems when you're thinking such thoughts!

I reckon that I'd walked just under a mile when I reached the end of the tunnel on the north bank of the Thames; I climbed up a staircase identical to the one I'd come down and emerged in front of the Tower of London.

These execrable monuments to human cruelty and misfortune always arouse a repulsion in me which is stronger than any curiosity, but I recalled the names of those who had died within its walls and forced myself to enter. The terrible memories crowd in as soon as you've passed the first enclosure. The castle is constructed in the form of a pentagon and is surmounted by eight towers, each one bringing to mind a famous prisoner and a wretched death. In one of the towers the sons of Edward IV were killed, in another Henry VI was assassinated, in a third the Duke of Clarence, brother to Edward IV, was drowned in a barrel. In the Bell Tower Queen Elizabeth was imprisoned, while in Beauchamp Tower Anne Boleyn passed her final days, as Lady Jane Grey did in the Brick Tower. A few steps further on, you reach the little square where secret executions took place where, among many other victims, Lady Jane Grey was beheaded. Nearby there is the little church where Anne Boleyn, Robert Devereux, Catherine Howard and others who were poisoned, stabbed or throttled in secret lie buried.

The exterior of the castle is bare and gloomy, and its interior is even more melancholy. Low-vaulted narrow steps lead to large bleak rooms and long dark corridors and sinister cells, those living tombs where so many wretches driven mad with despair tore their hair and beat their heads against the walls. The sight of the splendid armour worn by kings and princes on display in a ground-floor room distracts the mind for a while from such thoughts, but it soon relapses when we see the horrid dungeon where Elizabeth's favourite courtier, Walter Raleigh, languished for twelve years, or the axe and blood-stained block on which hundreds of the prisoners held in the Tower were beheaded; the still-intact instruments of torture which tore flesh and twisted bones but didn't kill. Cries which issue from our mouths only when our life is leaving us, horrifying groans, gestures and words of pleading supplication which tear the heart in twain, the superhuman endurance of men who do not want to die – all these you see and hear with the most vivid imagination as you walk round the inner recesses of this cursed building.

In a more remote room, kept in a great glass case surrounded by wire mesh, there is a heap of sceptres, diadems and bracelets which shine like an electric lamp. These are the diamonds of the British crown jewels, which all together are worth no less than seventy-five million lire.

On coming out of the Tower of London, I saw for the first time in a pub a man who was drunk on gin. I was horrified. I had no idea that drunkenness could transform a man in such a way. Back in Italy, drunkards who've put away a bit too much wine, whether they become boisterous or fall asleep, are – I'm almost tempted to say – a pleasant sight compared with these men, with their convulsed, disturbed faces and deathly pallor, their look of illness or madness and their eyes staring and fixed like a corpse's. And even in such a state you see these wretches go on gulping that tremendous liquor down their throats, collapsing to the ground as if they'd been hit by lightning, or witness the repulsive spectacle of them banging their heads against the wall or the table until the blood runs down their faces, while the bystanders watch and laugh.

But the sight of children in the streets and parks of London made up for the ugly spectacle of drunkards – those sweet English children who are, with reason, celebrated for being the freshest and best-behaved children in the world. You see blond heads of all shades – from the bright golden yellow of the English sovereign coin to the ash blond of the palest silk or the beard on a corncob – tumbling in large gleaming curls which tempt you to cut a scissorful of them as they pass by. Their cheeks come in all shades of pink, from the pale petals of the fully blossomed flower to the sweet little bud closed lovingly round the pistil; little mouths so crimson you're amazed the birds don't come to peck; blue eyes of an innocence to put the cherubs fluttering round Murillo's Madonnas* to shame. The only reason I didn't come back carrying an armful of these children is because I didn't know where I'd put them. But I couldn't resist the temptation, one day in Green Park, of grabbing hold of a little boy running past me and planting so many kisses on his cheeks he was breathless, and then returning him to his nurse who had run up to rescue him with a supplicatory gesture, as if to say, "Forgive me, I couldn't stop myself!"

The children remind me of my visit to the famous waxworks exhibition of Madame Tussaud. I don't regret going there, although the experience was more painful than pleasant. As soon as I had entered I found myself staring at the corpse of Napoleon III, laid out on a bed in the uniform of a field marshal, in so extraordinarily close a replica of the real thing that I was reluctant to go any nearer. While I was gazing at him I saw out of the corner of my eye a man standing next to me who was making a grief-stricken gesture. I turned to look at him and stepped back with a shudder: it was Pietri* – in wax – dressed all in black and standing upright in the middle of the crowd like a ghost. I breathed more freely in the large royal hall, where there were hundreds of kings and queens and generals, the entire courts of England and Spain, all dressed in splendid period costume. As I walked round the throne of some Aragonese king, I bumped into Thiers* with his tuft of hair sticking up; I squeezed between Kaiser Wilhelm and Prince Friedrich Karl and passed in front of Jules Favre* and Bismarck, who were having an animated conversation in a quiet corner. I hurried through the room dedicated to England's most notorious criminals: those savage and cretinous faces and furtive expressions, those clothes stained with blood – all in semi-darkness, which makes them seem almost real – horrified me. If someone behind a curtain had let out a scream I would easily have believed one of those murderers had plunged a knife into their heart.

One day I paid a visit to the famous Bank of England, which has a mere nine hundred employees on its staff, to whom it pays a trifling six million pounds in salaries, holds in its vaults the goodly sum of four hundred million pounds' worth of gold and silver and has on display in a glass case a note worth nothing less than twenty-five million. I entered the great hall where payments are made. A hundred clerks at a hundred counter windows dispensed silver and gold coins – in rolls, handfuls, spadefuls – with the rapidity of a magician performing tricks, while the creditors stuffed them hastily into pockets and bags and made their escape like thieves, casting distrustful glances around as they left. It's worth seeing the sudden looks, the brief smiles, the slight frowns or pursing of lips, the thousand eloquent and yet unfathomable expressions which cross the faces of those men as they see all that gold. And it's worth seeing the gold too – how it cascades, escapes, gleams, makes a ringing sound as if it's laughing merrily and slyly winks at you, like a living thing up to no good. Even I, watching that spectacle, felt for the very first time a guilty disturbance, and an expression passed across my face which, if anyone had seen it, would've prompted them to cry out: "Arrest that man!" When I was eighteen, I would never have felt such a thing. At that age you don't give any thought to not being wealthy. Youth is a time of mysterious expectations, as a great poet put it,* and among all the things you look forward to in a distant and indeterminate future, getting rich is merely one of them. There's a vague hope that unknown relatives will leave you a fortune or that one evening you'll come home from the theatre to find a wad of banknotes on your bedside table sent by some unknown benefactor. But each year that passes cancels out yet another of these fantasies conjured up by our imaginations, and so the sight of gold make us thoughtful and arouses melancholy longings – not for love of idleness but rather of the precious independence which the need for gainful employment takes away from us, of the possibility of spending ten years working on a book, of having four resident language tutors, of going off to explore Africa, of being able to offer our beloved a diadem of rubies and a palace of marble.

On the same day I also visited the famous Barclay's Brewery. The annual taxes it pays to the state amount to four and a half million lire, and year on year it consumes thirty million litres of barley. I wandered the streets of Southwark for some time looking for the entrance and finally asked someone, who told me, much to my astonishment, that I was already inside the brewery and had been walking around it the whole time. "You should call it a town, not a brewery!" I said to the guard who accompanied me. With English phlegm he just smiled, but demonstrated his gratitude by giving me detailed explanations and showing me round the endless labyrinth of the place, with its buildings, foaming lakes, gigantic barrels and splashing waterfalls of beer. When I asked him if we could take a rest he took me to sit on a high terrace from which, like a general surveying the battlefield, he swept his arm over the vast array of houses, warehouses, stables, granaries and courtyards which go to make up the site, proclaiming proudly, "Here is the greatest brewery on earth!"

That same evening I passed again by the Bank of England and saw the Stock Exchange, and for a while strolled about the tangle of streets vibrant with the city's trade. After I'd had my fill of the spectacle I returned to the hotel full of an entirely novel eagerness to take up business and acquire wealth. "Enough of being a writer!" I said to myself. "Action is what's needed! What's the point of spending one's life spinning words? All just empty rhetoric. Hard work, that's what's called for. Thank Heaven it's not too late for me. Lots of other people have gone into business later than me and made their fortunes. As soon as I'm back in Italy, I'll look for something, I'll find something to do. What if my friends mock me? Well, let them mock! I'll mock them when I build myself a villa in Fiesole. Now, let's think a little, what line of business should I go into? I need to start with something on a small scale... Wine, spirits... no, not really. Cotton..." But at that moment I thought I saw someone pointing a little white finger at me and asking in a teasing voice: "You?!" – so I too laughed and gave up my thoughts of going into trade.

4

YOU NEED TO BE RICH to visit the museums of London properly – in other words, you would need to set up home in London for an entire year. If you haven't got the time, the visits are nothing more than forced marches. It seems to me I'm still running through the interminable rooms of that universal emporium otherwise known as the South Kensington Museum, in the continual hope, each time I enter a new room, that this one will be the last, only to find, to my stupefaction, that another sequence of rooms stretches before me. It's already a lot that I recall the famous cartoons of Raphael or a marvellous portrait of Hamlet by Lawrence which stopped me dead in one of the corridors to ask me the awesome enigma. But the small museum of paintings in Trafalgar Square doesn't have this disadvantage: I can still remember as freshly as when I set eyes on them Hogarth's immortal story of a wedded couple for which he was paid two thousand lire and which was sold for twenty times as much fifty years later; Turner's stupendous battles of light; the Raphael paintings I'd wanted to see for twenty-five years; and the pictures by the four painters most loved by the English – Correggio, Poussin, Murillo and Claude Lorrain. But it was back to forced marches in the India Museum, the Soane Museum, the Maritime Museum, the Royal College of Surgeons (where you can see the skeletons of Caroline Crachami, the celebrated Sicilian dwarf who was so small you could have buried her inside a top hat, and of Byrne, the Irish giant who when he walked along the streets could light the pipes of people leaning out of the window on the first floor).

My most vivid impression however remains of the Chamber of the House of Commons. I entered it without realizing where I was – it was empty at the time – but even when I'd taken a good look at it, it never entered my head it might be the parliamentary chamber. It seems very small and is magnificently decorated with aristocratic taste, like a cathedral choir for elegant canons or a place of assembly for fair-haired, white-robed countesses. When I discovered it was the Commons chamber – home of the unruffled simple eloquence of the world's greatest orators, an eloquence echoed and diminished in the pompous pronouncements and pedantic citations found in the parliaments of the Latin countries – I bowed my head respectfully and asked permission to touch the Mace with the tips of my fingers in the hope that it would instil in me the un-Latin virtue of calm discussion.

As a rest from the laborious visits to museums and palaces, I would go to the parks – great oases in the populous desert of London, where your spirit is cheered to see that the world isn't entirely made up of buildings and railways. Hundreds of beautiful women riding beautiful horses down avenues which stretch out of sight and thousands of children scattered racing over the vast lawns and around the great ponds crossed by innumerable toy sailing boats make you realize with pleasure that life is not all traffic and labour, while the abundant greenery, the cheerful faces and the melodious sounds of Italian music evoke, with a tender longing, the image of your dear motherland which you will soon see again. O Hyde Park and Regents Park, Victoria and St James's, the parks of Greenwich, Southwark, Battersea, Holland Park – kind comforters for my melancholia – I thank you and greet you! And I also remember gratefully Windsor's Castle Hill, the woods of Eton, the walks in

Richmond and the gardens in Kew and all the pleasant
outskirts of the city where I escaped the lethal ennui of
Sunday afternoons. If you have not experienced London on
a Sunday you don't know what boredom is. Closed doors,
shuttered windows, empty streets, silent squares; entire
neighbourhoods abandoned, where you could die of hunger
without anyone helping or even noticing; the bleakness of
uninhabited towns and an infinite tedium hanging over
everything; even the statues seem sleepy and the very houses
look bored, and your violent yawns are so wide and long you
immediately check to see you haven't dislocated your jaw.

London seemed to get bigger and bigger each day I was
there. However far I walked in any direction I never suc-
ceeded in finding the point where the city finished, not even
a thinning out of houses which suggested it was coming to
an end. Walking through certain areas for a second time
I came across whole neighbourhoods as large as Florence
which had escaped my attention the first time round. Every
day, even just within the West End, which was the area I most
frequented, I would find, as if by magic, huge streets I hadn't
even spotted on the map. I'd set out in the morning, going
past places I'd visited the previous day, without recognizing

them; I'd arrive in a park where I would rest to get my breath back and restore my courage; and then off I'd set again in the infinite labyrinth of streets on foot, by bus, in a hansom cab, with an exclamation of surprise every time I turned a corner like someone reaching the top of a mountain and suddenly finding a whole new country below him. My head is still full of a thousand confused images of crossroads thronged with people, vast empty spaces and misty distances – where they were or when I saw them I have no idea – which often merge into the visions of imaginary cities we see in our dreams.

London's size and wealth had a different effect on me all the time. My native pride as an Italian sometimes felt crushed; I would scornfully recall the petty boasts we allow ourselves in our own country, when all we have to compare ourselves with is ourselves; I decided, on my return, to rebut such boasts with sarcasm. I wished I'd been born an Englishman so I could look down on the Latin races. At other times, instead, the spectacle of English superiority made my affection for my own country even keener, mixed with tender compassion. Does a child love his mother less, I thought, because she is poor and sickly? But frequently, too, the superiority of the English didn't seem to me to be enviable. Vanity, all vanity, I said to myself. Like Leopardi's shepherd, I wondered what the purpose was of all this movement, this vast agitation of people and things. Are the English happier than we are? So what if they're wealthier? at least we haven't got any fog and a poor wretch in the sunshine perhaps enjoys his life more than a rich man in the gloom. And is it not the case that here too infinite pain and suffering are to be found? And sometimes being Italian was a source of self-esteem. Occasionally on the bus a fellow passenger, on learning that I was Italian, would look at me with a mixture of kindliness and curiosity as if to see whether they could find something in my face which matched that vague image of beauty and happiness which the name of Italy conjures up in all foreigners, and I would be filled with pleasure, and glimpse from my reflection in the window that my eyes were shining and my cheeks were blushing.

It is indeed true that travel teaches us modesty! To the person who travels, how narrow the habitual round of his knowledge and his ideas appears – even if at home, among his friends and books, it seemed so wide! To discover that at least half of all the learning we've managed to acquire in years of study and observation is worth almost nothing when we visit a foreign land! To feel on our pulses the truth that when we were at home and thought we were reading the book of the world, all we were really reading was a mere page, that all the things which seemed to us so large and important that they filled half the globe are nothing more than knick-knacks, not worth a farthing once we step outside our door! It's as if with every step we take in a foreign country a crevice opens up under our eyes, in which we see the abyss of our ignorance and from whose depths a laugh of compassion rises up. But there are also moments when, by contrast, ideas move rapidly in our heads and when we see, guess, understand in a flash all kinds of things which were unknown and obscure to us before – if this febrile activity of the mind would remain and continue, what extraordinary men we would be! What great designs we embark on at such moments, which vanish in thin air at the next turn in the road!

After its size and wealth, what I found most extraordinary in London was its orderliness. The whole enormous city is as neat as a Dutch village. The various operations of its vast life run like clockwork. A foreigner who can barely understand two words of French can manage, by himself, to deal with any difficulty and without wasting a minute of his time. The street walls and the buses are covered with an infinite number of signs which constantly and at every step tell you which direction you need to go in. If someone loses his way in London, all he has to do, whichever part of the city he's in, is to follow the direction of the first train he sees moving among the roofs above him; the train will lead him to a station; at the station he'll find directions on the wall on how to get home. One day I boarded a bus without knowing where it was going. It took me many miles outside London. I got out at a country inn, on my own. None of the people in the inn understood a word of French; I couldn't find out where I was and when the next bus would depart. I became slightly worried. I took a turn around the village – spotless cottages with little gardens all spick and span, the only people to be seen an aristocratic-looking youth on horseback and some fair-haired young lady glimpsed behind a window, everything as silent as a graveyard. What should I do? Where should I go? Suddenly I heard a puff of steam, as heart-warming as the voice of a friend; I ran towards it and in fifteen minutes was back in London.

The evenings in London for a foreigner are very depressing. A ferocious melancholy would descend on me. I'd grown used to the splendour of Parisian boulevards and the festive crowds which throng them; the streets of London seemed dark and gloomy by comparison. I missed the packed cafés, the sumptuous shops, and even the magic-lantern shows on the boulevard Montmartre, conveniently forgetting the indignation I also felt at the sight of the brazen and ostentatious prostitution which is rife all over Paris. But how strange these moments of discouragement are, these deep feelings of sadness which overcome us in the evenings in an unfamiliar city! So deep that sometimes passers-by look at your face and take pity on you! But why? you ask yourself – you're in good health, you're not short of money, the news from home is good, you're free, you'll enjoy yourself tomorrow morning, in ten days' time you'll be back in your own country: so why this suicidal mien? Who knows? Like the leper in de Maistre's novel,* I too, when I've passed in the street a married couple with children and a nurse pushing a pram, all smiling and happy, have felt a bitter envy rising within me and have looked away.

It is possible in London, if you've got a letter of introduction, to obtain permission to accompany the police on their nightly round in the most squalid areas of the city, swarming with criminals and beggars, and penetrate the hovels where those wretches, with barely a penny to their name, go to spend the night. I visited these neighbourhoods only during the daytime, walking among the opium dens where people go to drug themselves, the places where you pay a penny to see obscene dances or where lovers of boxing go to watch heavy punches flying, eyes being bruised and teeth broken; where you find women with their heads split open by their drunken husbands; where the wasted whore embraces the blood-stained thief; where prostitution is a trade begun in childhood and continued till old age; where cruelty, lust and poverty, coupling like unclean monsters, lurk in the shadows and wait to send their victims to drown in the Thames or to the hospitals or to the scaffold; where, in short, all the filth of the great city ferments, and where Charles Dickens went to drink beer with his servant.

The finest morning I spent in London was the last, culminating in the most entertaining cosmopolitan gathering there's ever been. I had climbed the Monument built by Wren – the famous tower which commemorates the Great Fire which burnt down four hundred and sixty streets and fourteen thousand houses – from the summit of which you can see with one glance all the traffic round London Bridge and the network of streets on the south bank of the Thames. I found five friendly young men up at the top, massacring the French language (except for one of them) as they talked away cheerfully with the casualness of barbershop assistants. After we'd exchanged a few words I discovered to my great pleasure that one of them came from Cologne, one from Manchester, one from Harlem, one from Guadalajara and the fifth from Lyon, so that, together with me, we represented six nations – Germany, England, France, Italy, Spain and Holland – three Latin and three Nordic peoples, four healthy monarchies and two sick republics. We laughed over the curious encounter, since the German and the Dutchman had also just arrived by chance a few minutes before I had, while the other three had come across each other the day before. With the serious air of an international commission summoned to resolve some dispute, we went off to have lunch together. Except for the Spaniard and, in part, the Italian, the others drank like fishes; the table was soon covered with empty glasses, and the conversation grew very lively. The beer fumes had dissolved away all political hatreds and malice and aroused instead in all six of us a sentiment of universal love which was proclaimed in loud toasts to the prosperity and glory of all our nations, *quoique indignement*, as the man from Lyon said in that spirited conference which should *servir d'exemple aux gouvernements*. Before we'd ordered the eighth bottle, Alsace had been restored, all fears that war might break out over the Roman question dissipated, the Carlists on the French border put in handcuffs, and Luxembourg's independence against German claims secured for all time to come. Then there entered on stage – on the dining table – Gutenberg, Coster, Michelangelo, Mendoza, Newton, William of Orange, Victor Hugo – on whom were showered a series of adjectives appropriate to the dessert course washed down with more wine: divine, immense, sublime, superhuman. Then, as our familiarity with each other grew, the conversation grew more personal – "I'm a shopkeeper" – "I'm a journalist" – "I… manage to get by" – and we asked each other's ages and mutually complimented each other – "What a fine figure of a German you are!" and "What a fine figure of an Italian you are!" and to mangle each others' languages, and every now and then someone would shout "But we've run out of drink!" – and then there's talk of grand plans and agreements to meet up again next year in Paris, in Amsterdam, in Constantinople, in such a street, on such a day, at such a time; and "I'll be there!" and "Write to me" and "Take care!" – and then a final clinking together of brimming glasses to the cry of "Long live civilization!"

At midday near the Tower of London I boarded a steamship bound for Antwerp.

The extraordinary expanse of London can only be completely appreciated by travelling up and down the Thames. London Bridge and the City shrink in comparison with the port: indeed the whole of London seems to diminish in size.

The sun shone and the sky was clear as the ship departed. It steamed between two rows of large ships. In a few minutes we were clear of St Katherine Dock, which extends over a space where once twelve thousand people had their dwellings and is now the port where ships from Germany, the Low Countries, France and Scotland arrive. We left behind the London Docks, where the basins hold three hundred tall-sided ships and the warehouses contain two hundred thousand tons of merchandise, and travelled rapidly on, alongside ships, tugboats, barges, vessels of every type going

Watering cart in London

The new London Bridge

up and down the broad river. For a while there's nothing remarkable about the spectacle. There are huge piles and long rows of sacks and barrels and crates and bales covering the banks and jetties and bridges and the entrances to roads; immensely long boundary walls and rows of dark houses, and everywhere the smoke of factories, moving machinery, workmen and sailors at their business, all the varied to-ing and fro-ing which you see in any great port. Except that, when you reach the great bend in the Thames and you begin to say that never before have you travelled so long a stretch of water in the midst of ships, once past the bend, as you see the new stretch of river ahead of you with masts and sails as far as the eye can reach, you are completely astounded. But that's not all, since then you realize that beyond the masts and sails, beyond the high walls which extend along the banks of the river, there are forests - dense, deep, labyrinthine forests - of ships. To the left there are the great basins of the West India Docks, covering a hundred hectares; to the right there are the five great Commercial and Surrey docks, which extend for several miles inland. We're no longer moving through two rows of ships but through two rows of ports, too large for the gaze to take in. Once past the Commercial docks, we travel on for several miles in the midst of lesser docks, but still with forests of ships, black-walled warehouses as large as towns and stacks of merchandise. We pass in front of the glorious hospital of Greenwich and turn at the Isle of Dogs. We've already been travelling for two hours, the ships are fewer in number, and although there's still no break in the line of warehouses, factories, houses along the two banks, it seems as if the port is coming to an end. You take a breath, you need a rest, you're tired of being continually in a state of astonishment. Another hour passes, and London already seems like a remote city and the bustle and noise of the port as if remembered from yesterday. Then, suddenly, at another turn in the river, new lines of ships appear, new forests of masts and rigging, new docks of immense size, another port, another extraordinary spectacle. One's astonishment changes into stupor; it's as though you're dreaming or as if you're entering another London. You pass alongside the East India docks, the arsenal at Woolwich and the Victoria docks, which stretch for three miles along the left bank, and so on amid endless walls, endless numbers of ships, goods, machines, clouds of smoke, whistles, departures, arrivals, flags from all the nations on earth, faces of all colours, words of unknown languages which you hear as you pass alongside ships, strange costumes and wild cries which flash before your imagination the prospect of distant oceans and remote shores. The spectacle lasts for three hours! Your sense of wonder might be exhausted, but wonder again you must. Your mind feels exalted; no longer do you feel that sense of humiliation you experienced at the beginning, comparing this country to your own. It's no longer a question of comparing; you become cosmopolitan; national pride is extinguished, to be replaced by human pride; this is no longer the port of London, but the port of every country, the centre of world commerce, the meeting place of peoples of every race and from every part of the globe; and while the gaze takes in the spectacle, one's thoughts travel across the continents and see the vast curves over the earth's surface made by the myriad ships which pass and salute each other; the infinite effort and danger involved, the endless criss-crossing of land and sea, the eternal labour of indefatigable humanity. You seem for the first time to understand the laws governing the life of the world. Meanwhile the steamer speeds on its way, the Thames widens, the forests of ships seem like vast reedbeds against the horizon lit by the setting sun; but there are yet more docks, basins, warehouses and arsenals. London, the great city, is still with us; after four hours of navigation, it still follows us; on the left, on the right, ahead, as far as the eye can reach, you see, with a mixture almost of misgiving and fear, the monstrous city which never ceases to work and to expand.

An Excursion to the Poor Districts of London

Louis Laurent Simonin

I

*How I found myself in London – project for an
excursion to the poor districts – Seven Dials – Mr
Price, the police inspector – a procession of beggars*

I T WAS JUNE 1862. I happened to be in London with
my friend Monsieur D.B.,* a painter, and one of his
students. We had just returned from the mines of Cornwall
and the very peculiar industrial areas of Wales, a picturesque
excursion whose incidents, to date unpublished, are being
reserved for *Around the World.*

At that time in London there were ten times more foreigners than usual; everyone was at the Great Exhibition
which, for the second time in eleven years, was gathering
within its walls the peoples and products of the entire
world.

I had made many previous visits to the nave and the tran-
septs, the galleries and annexes of the Palace of Kensington,
and admired the specimens of industry from one or other
hemisphere, brought together there in such a short space

77

of time as if by the waving of a fairy wand. My friends followed me to begin with but, sooner wearied than I by this unvarying spectacle, they lost no time in seeking other diversions in London. However, the queen of cities, to name her as the English do, soon showed the foreigner all that she had to offer. She is far from capable of giving him all the amusements, all the joys, of Paris. So what were we to do? Run to the brightest lights, like most tourists. Nevertheless, we did not take our leave in an outburst of splenetic resentment, but having decided to look closely at everything around us that might excite our curiosity, we determined to make an excursion into the poor districts of London.

The gloomy nooks and crannies of Whitechapel, Wapping and Christchurch are less known – not only to the French, but even to the Londoners themselves – than the harem in Constantinople. In these sad recesses, crammed on top of each other, swarm all those disadvantaged by fate, all those with neither hearth nor home, who have been led here by vice and misery. There you will find thieves mingling with the crowd of unfortunates, those famous pickpockets dodging the English police, who are the craftiest force in the universe. There pallid youth rots: girls and boys without parents, children of chance, made old before their time by moral debasement, neglect and hunger.

The location of these districts of classic misery, to which we must add that of St George-in-the-East, isolates them, we might say, in the very heart of London. They are at the easternmost point of the great metropolis, bounded on one side (the south) by the Thames – or, if you prefer, by the Tower of London, the port and docks; and on the other side (the west) by the City, that turbulent centre of business.

London is the city of contrasts. It has been said, with good reason, that in the capital of the three kingdoms there are only the rich and the poor. It is beside the City, near the points from which flow all the treasures of the world, in the vicinity of the Customs House, the Bank, the Mint and the docks, that the most wretched parts of that immense city are to be found.

To the east and north, the borders of these districts are indistinct; they end where misery ends. Indeed, to the north misery is prolonged, and it could be said that Bethnal Green is a sad continuation of Whitechapel.

So we had all the material we needed for an exploration, even a sort of investigation if necessary; but first we wanted to sound out the terrain like soldiers on active service.

We had been told that it was unwise to go off in such an impromptu fashion into these remote places so little visited by respectable people, to venture so lightly, even in broad daylight, into these labyrinths with no way out, known only to those who lived there, and from which we were certain to depart relieved of all our belongings. We took account of this advice, and considered it appropriate, before setting off into Whitechapel, to study another district which resembled it in miniature. So we went on our voyage of discovery one morning, alone, trusting in our kind stars, to the area known as Seven Dials, a stain on the centre of London like a great inkblot on a sheet of smooth white paper. If Seven Dials is not quite enclosed within the aristocratic districts, it is nonetheless only ten steps from Regent Street and Piccadilly, two centres of elegant society, of "fashion", as they say on that side of the straits.

Seven Dials is in fact the name given to a small, almost circular square, at whose perimeter seven streets (seven dials) converge and give it its name. Go into any one of these streets and you will see that the biting portrait of Seven

Dials drawn by one of Britain's greatest novelists and most acute observers – Charles Dickens, writing then under the pseudonym of Boz, is truly taken from nature.

What filthy mud in these foul streets, what heaps of rubbish! What wretched shops, where piles of old discarded items gathered from who knows where, harvested who knows how, are spread out in the vain hope of a sale: hideous, garish rags, rust-eaten ironmongery, half-rotten bones, clothes and shoes from some antediluvian era. A sickening smell is emitted by these lowly hovels – and then come some pestilent taverns, whose exhalations of gin and brandy catch in your throat, and in which one can glimpse through a half-open door a thick layer of blackish, gleaming grime left there by the patrons of the place. This new variety of glue has fastened itself to plasterwork and wood, rendering everything uniform. Beside the taverns there are open-air stalls where nameless fried dishes and mismatched pieces of meat from who knows what beast await the day's passing trade; then, here and there, long, narrow, gloomy alleyways filled with a kind of mystery; staircases sometimes opening right onto the street, their steps never visited by a broom, half worn through, sunken, often incomplete, real traps for those who do not know these dangerous passageways. Pieces of cloth of any random kind are hung at the windows, and items of laundry dangle from a cord to dry. Whatever substance is used on these sordid tatters has the remarkable effect of making them seem still dirtier, so much have they lost their original colours.

So where are the inhabitants of this beggars' neighbour-hood, this new Court of Miracles?* The inhabitants are asleep. Apart from a few tradesmen standing in front of their shops, and a few rare passers-by who give us a hard stare and see very clearly that we are not local, the place is deserted, silent, which is all the more astonishing as it is so near to Covent Garden market, one of the busiest areas in London. Some houses seem boarded up, some shops are actually closed. I made my surprise clear to D.B., who is making a quick sketch, and all of a sudden I heard a voice answering me in good French: "Ah, Monsieur, you should come here between ten in the evening and three in the morning, and then you'll truly see a crowd! In this neighbourhood people work by night and sleep by day."

Responding to this interjection, I became aware of an old woman who, having heard and understood me, was finding nothing better to do than to insert herself with great familiarity into the conversation. Her accent and the facility with which she expressed herself indicated she was French. How had she ended up, and at her age, among these revolting hovels? Could she guide us, conduct us, show us around? I was on the point of asking her all this, and of heaping other questions upon her, when in an instant she slipped away from me and disappeared down the end of an alley, where I tried in vain to track her down. Perhaps the old woman had a guilty conscience and, before such curious compatriots, thought it more prudent to make herself scarce. In any case, we had been advised: it was at night that we should visit this resort of theft and misery. We should go there as one goes to a concert or a play, and we immediately planned a great excursion for the next evening.

Whitechapel was the focal point of our curiosity, the most picturesque place to explore, even though the half-glimpsed Seven Dials, St Giles (where fifty thousand Irishmen were crammed) and Bethnal Green, the weavers' quarter, were not to be overlooked. So we settled on Whitechapel and its environs, and went that very day to the local police station situated on Leman Street to ask the inspector, Mr Price, for permission to visit the places of interest of his district.

To start with, Mr Price, with true English strictness, asked for our names, first names and professions and, when he had understood the purpose of our peregrination, said to us graciously, "Come and see me at ten o'clock tomorrow evening. I shall show you everything, you shall see it all. You could not be in better hands, for you are with the police inspector responsible for common lodging houses."

And when we asked him if we should dress to fit in, he answered, "Have no fear. Dress in your usual manner. Look out for your watches and pocketbooks. In the company of myself and my men, no one shall lay a hand on you, and you shall lose nothing. Even in places where you may be stripped of all your belongings in broad daylight, no one shall dare to touch a hair on your head. Come, I shall show you the resorts of thieves and fallen women, their taverns, their theatres, their places of entertainment, the prisons where we heap up those persons taken by night on the public highway, the places where sailors, labourers, jugglers and crooks all lodge together; and lastly the abandoned hovels where tramps and beggars, numb with cold and dying of hunger, find a few hours' rest, and sometimes their final shelter."

Inspector Price's description promised a most interesting tour, and we assured him that we would not fail to meet him as agreed. We were in Whitechapel and, prompted by curiosity, after a walk of quite some distance, we did not wish to return to our lodgings without glancing at the scarcely appetizing stalls of Butchers' Street and the rag fair which is held in Houndsditch. The inhabitants of these fine places, however little they may care for the picturesque, may rightly take pride in these two displays. The produce on show certainly does rival that of the Great Exhibition, but it does not lack charm of another sort. Besides, in this situation we were favoured beyond the common degree of fortune in seeing the very strange population of these districts in broad daylight and in all its aspects, as is given to very few tourists. A wretched girl was being buried, having been stabbed seven times in a jealous rage by a sailor who then killed himself. This funeral had affected the entire neighbourhood, and the streets of Whitechapel and Leman and all their adjoining roads were overflowing. How many battered black hats, filthy jackets, down-at-heel and mismatched boots we saw pass by is impossible to say; likewise the women, young and old, in faded hats, in plaid shawls adorned with holes and hideous stains, and the children in grimy tatters! No stocking or shirt in sight, everywhere heads of hair that had never seen a comb, untended beards where the dust lay at ease, where wisps of straw and threads of cotton were fixed like nests. Skin showed everywhere through the rents in their clothes – a dark, earth-coloured skin with the pores blocked. Filthiness has its benefits: this impermeable skin puts a stop to perspiration, which soon ceases entirely, so that one may economize on daily bread, which does not always come when it is due. Who could ever tell all that we saw on that memorable day, which made a festival for Whitechapel, that parade of misery, of degradation, in that colourful crowd assembling with anxious curiosity, at the burial of a girl of low character murdered by her lover? Who could paint that procession of haggard, crazed, fierce, discoloured faces? Not even Homer numbering his Grecian warriors made a list to equal that one in length; never did Callot* paint such realistic beggars, so poorly clad as ours.

2

*The Prince of Denmark; the guests pay at the
dance hall – a pension for sailors – a dormitory for
labourers – the thieves' taproom – an expansive
pickpocket – low bedrooms – a conjurer chang-
ing silver into copper – nocturnal tableaux – three
poor girls – a well-attended prison – a glance at the
Thames – Haymarket at dawn – wretched London
and its visitors – remedies for pauperism*

T HE NEXT DAY we arrived at the appointed hour at Leman Street police station, where Inspector Price was waiting for us. With him were two officers in civilian clothes and a third in uniform: stiff hat of waxed hessian, black jacket with silver buttons, black trousers, and under the sleeve of his jacket the sacred baton, the truncheon which characterizes the English bobby. In addition to this, each of these gentlemen was equipped in addition with one of those muffled lamps that can be hidden under the clothing, a precious piece of equipment without which the London constable never ventures out at night.

A friend having accompanied us, we were eight in number, counting Mr Price and his three officers, and with a pair of eyes watching over each one of us we could proceed in tranquillity. We marched along the pavement in silence two by two. Soon, leaving Leman Street, which is broad and well paved – for it may be remarked that in the poor quarters of London one comes upon great arteries which might be the envy of less miserable districts – we made our way into a maze of narrow winding streets. These streets, almost deserted by day, were now highly animated.

All the shops were lit up, the bars full to the very doors, so that there was often a queue of drinkers. At almost every step we encountered groups of labourers or sailors, singing or quarrelling, half drunk. At the street corners, pale blonde girls, whose beauty sometimes equalled their youth, but very poorly dressed, barefooted, hair in disarray, breasts scarcely covered, accosted passers-by in hoarse voices. However, there was in all this a certain order, a certain calm, and one could guess that the hour for the vile saturnalia had not yet sounded, and that we were still only at the beginning.

Mr Price, to encourage us to patience, led us into Grace's Alley, to the Prince of Denmark, a vast establishment set up as a theatre. At the door we were recognized as police and admitted without tickets. The Prince of Denmark is a café with singing and dancing, and is much frequented: there are performing dogs and monkeys, and tumblers execute their numbers on trapeze and high wire. All this entertained us for a moment. The patrons of the place showed great interest in the performances, and we found nothing in the dress or appearance of the spectators which seemed out of the ordinary. Clearly Mr Price intended to proceed gradually. Indeed, it was not long before we saw other such music halls, where foreign sailors, mingling with shameless women, served as both performers and audience.

In one of these halls, a dancer of the utmost agility wished to show us a specimen of the British jig. It was wonderful to see this young man shimmying about on the platform until he was quite out of breath. A circle formed around him; nobody among his comrades, the young girls in dancing costumes or the older women, missed a single one of the dancer's leaps. We had to await the close. Then came the rounds of applause and congratulations, after which we were offered beer and punch, and so graciously that we were obliged to accept. "Howl with the wolves," as they say. So we

Jig in a music hall

The trickster of Montague Street

clinked glasses with the ladies who had come to sit beside us for a moment, without their companions taking the least offence. We had no wish, for our own part, to look insulted. Withdrawing, we even paid for what we had drunk, which earned us the singular honour of being accompanied to the street by our new acquaintances and having the epithet of "gentlemen" bestowed upon us. We could hardly be much charmed by all these marks of attention, given the character of the persons by whom they were proffered; but we had to endure it, and Mr Price had seen all this many times before. Besides, he wished to conceal nothing from us, and showed us the most hideous houses of these coarse districts. We were greatly surprised to encounter a calm and propriety generally unknown in these low places. We even found that the miserable creatures inhabiting these sad crannies seemed to have a feeling of shame about their situation; they blushed in the presence of their unexpected visitors, and answered our questions shamefacedly with bowed heads.

The police, who were watching over us with paternal benevolence, then led us to the hotels of the area. We began by visiting a guest house with furnished rooms for sailors in Well Close Square. I need hardly tell you that the gentlemen lodging there were at the moment all absent, toasting Bacchus, in spite of the late hour inclining one to sleep. The master of the house, John Seymour, took great pride in showing us his rooms like a well-versed cicerone. "You can see how everything is perfectly arranged," he said, "and how I have taken full advantage of the space. At sea, my fellows only sleep on hammocks; here they have proper closets." And he showed, almost obscured amid the apartment's wood panelling, a set of enormous chests of drawers without fronts: these were the sailor's beds. "Look... look here," he went on, revealing yet more, "these are excellent value, since each one has its own straw mattress, sheet and blanket. The cost is three pence (three centimes) a night, and every occupant has a number." And indeed, Master John was quite right: considering the price which the sleepers paid, the house was in very good order.*

Having started to show us the living quarters, Mr Price wanted to introduce us to that kind of order that the English seek in everything, and led us to East London Chambers. This vast establishment, which contains nothing but rooms for labourers, occupies seven houses in Wentworth Street. Its arrangement is truly remarkable: in the dining rooms there are separate booths, as in the best class of restaurant, where each person may take his meal unseen by his neighbour. As we know, in certain public places the English love to be cooped up like horses in a stable. The Anglo-Saxon is an eager practitioner of isolation; his best friend is undoubtedly *himself*.

In the rooms a number of beds are arranged in rows against the wall. A small room for ablutions is to be found on each floor. A kitchen on the ground floor is available for those who wish to prepare their own meals. In the common hall there is an enormous hearth with a fire always lit. Here and there inscriptions hang from the walls urging propriety in action and word, and instructing boxers to practise their art elsewhere. William Poole, the proprietor of this exemplary establishment, showed it to us with a certain pride. It remains to be seen if the demeanour of the guests matches the good order of the house. It is hardly probable, for none of his tenants had yet returned to his lodgings at the unseasonable hour of our visit.

Midnight had struck long ago; both the drinking places and the streets were filling with an ever greater, and far from reassuring crowd. A few good-for-nothings brushed against us as they passed and examined us coldly from the corner of their eyes, as if to estimate the profit that might be made from us, but, recognizing the police, they quickly assumed an air of indifference, some even going so far as to greet Mr Price politely and addressing him by name.

In one taproom which we entered, "a den of thieves" according to the inspector – noisy, lively, with some distinctive groups of patrons – Mr Price was once more recognized, greeted and made much of. A thief came up to him. I can still see him: he was a small, thin man, hideous, with thinning hair, unkempt beard, red hesitant eyes without lashes, bloodshot with alcohol. His face was crisscrossed with wrinkles, his nose split – no doubt broken like Michelangelo's by a punch – his skin as colourless as soiled parchment.

"Oh! Here you are then, my dear Mr Price," he said to the inspector. "Are you quite well?"

And he took the inspector's hand in two of his own and kissed it.

"Our good Mr Price, our dear inspector!" he cried, showing him to his comrades, and seeming tempted to call him the father of thieves, a godsend to pickpockets.

Mr Price let him do as he wished, calmly, impassively, always with the dignity of a true Englishman and, above all, of a police inspector; but he seemed to be saying to himself, "One more trick from you, my lad, and just see if I don't have you. Let me catch you with your hand in someone else's pocket, and you'll find out if the police can be softened up with two-faced caresses."

The other thieves, though somewhat less demonstrative, also gathered around Mr Price. They seemed to have a sort of deference towards him, a filial respect. Some of them, a little the worse for drink, even went so far as to offer him a glass of whisky at the bar. Among the whole crowd there was perhaps not a single man with whom Mr Price or his officers had not had dealings; all were known to be nimble-fingered thieves, but they had to be caught in flagrante, and while this event was awaited they were permitted to drink and ply their trade, since they could not be arrested before.

On leaving the taproom, a favourite haunt of pickpockets, which far excels the cabaret of the White Rabbit, not long ago a well-known feature of Les Fèves,* and so highly celebrated by *The Mysteries of Paris*, we made our way to Flower and Dean Street. These refined names contrast strikingly with the place we were about to visit. It was a hideous boarding house, principally a lodging for tramps, beggars, prostitutes and thieves; so Mr Price whispered in my ear as he discreetly raised the door knocker. A tottering old porter came to admit us, still on duty at this late hour, for these districts turn night into day, and no doubt a fine is levied against those who come home too early. A few rare sleepers were stretched out in the bedrooms and did not wake at our approach. From their gasping noise as they breathed, the booming snores of one, the convulsive jerking of another, which interrupted the sleep of a third, it might be guessed that each one was sleeping off the effects of a recent orgy. In every case it was a sleep troubled by dreams, agitated by the vapours of gin, brandy, ale or porter, incendiary liquors so dear to British gullets. The condition of the establishment was in harmony with that of its patrons: the stairwell was a veritable trap, the walls dreadfully greasy and, worst of all, a noxious odour, *sui generis*, was exhaled by every room and corridor, an odour of grimy old clothes, rank old boots, rotten rags and the most nauseating things that might be imagined. We could not bear it any longer and asked to leave the place. On our

Young beggars sleeping

way out, we cast an eye into the refectory, where, slumped on benches or lying on the floor, clustered like down-and-outs in Murillo, poor, almost naked children were sleeping.

These little tramps, whose parents were undoubtedly "out at work" at this hour, were starting out in a life of misery, abandonment and ignorance. Children promised to vice and the prisons, worthy sons of their fathers! After this, who can be astonished that pauperism extends its ravages ever further through London, and that in spite of so many charitable institutions, vagabondage, beggary, theft, degradation and murder have so many adepts in the modern Babylon!

If Flower and Dean Streets offer such indecent lodgings, what shall I say about those of Lower Keate Street, frequented by dangerous thieves "of the most expert class" as Mr Price designated them, being one who knew them well? Here dwell pickpockets of European renown, who systematically bleed London and all of Britain, planning their attacks far in advance like fine chess players, entire communities of crooks with their commanders and their statutes, who from to time leave the cities of the United Kingdom to go and trouble Paris or Vienna with their audacious thievery.

Let us throw a veil over these haunts of rascals which the police only authorize and tolerate in order to lay their mousetraps more easily, and let us take the reader to Montague Street, where we shall find a series of seemingly more respectable lodging houses. These are hotels where conjurers, tricksters, acrobats, gypsies and buskers, that whole interloping world which follows the fairs and races, come to lodge. We spent a pleasant quarter of an hour there, and one of the habitués of the place, who was warming himself peacefully in the common hall instead of sleeping in his bed, even though it was three in the morning, wanted to give us a sample of his skills. In our presence he performed some card tricks using beakers and sleight of hand, which were not without some merit. The most ingenious consisted in knotting into the corner of a handkerchief a shilling (one franc twenty-five centimes), which he had requested from one of us, then untying the knot to reveal instead of our silver coin a large copper penny (ten centimes), which he presented to us with that exquisite courtesy that is peculiar to conjurers. We accepted with good grace this transmutation of metals repeated before us many times over, and to our cost, in a method contrary to that of the alchemists, who at least tried to change copper into silver and lead into gold, base metals into noble ones, as they used to say in the good old days of the bellows-blowers. However, we took our leave well satisfied by the conjurer, and the conjurer still more satisfied by us.

Thus, mingling the comic with the serious, we passed through these strange districts under the vigilant eye of the police, who never let us out of their sight. With what fatherly care those good constables guided us! With what unity of purpose they directed us across sordid alleys, gloomy court-yards, passageways which one might have thought lacked any way out! We guessed that our very lives were in their hands. Without their constant vigilance we would surely have been stripped of our shirts (begging the pardon of the English for uttering that all too apposite word), and even of our scarves, had we attempted to defend ourselves. The faces we encountered seemed to be veiled by clouds. Sodden with drink, the villains whose domain we were traversing started to grope their way home. Here they lay full-length against a wall and would not stand up again till daybreak; there they collapsed upon a heap of refuse into which they half-disappeared; others stuck fast in the mud or slipped in the stream, whose cool water, stroking their faces and limbs, revived them for a moment. These opened a wild eye and called out to the passer-by in an unintelligible language. Not all the walkers were drunk, and more than one of the nocturnal "workers", having a steely resolve, had resisted the effects of a more than prolonged drinking session. Some marched by in noisy groups, singing coarse refrains in the unmusical voice typical of most Englishmen. Others, lurking in doorways, conversed in low voices and seemed to be up to no good. As the police passed, they instantly fell silent and made a show of setting off on a walk.

As we were confronted with this hideous world, we arrived at the filthiest alley we had yet traversed. Through a wide-open door we entered a wooden hovel whose disjointed boards gave free admittance to the outside air. No lamp helped us climb the staircase. We held on to each other's coat-tails and followed the first policeman who showed the way with his lantern. Through a half-open door in a foul den on the first floor, we saw two men lying in the same bed, and two bandit faces shot ferocious glares at us, growling and cursing at being awoken by these "French dogs" and sending our impertinent curiosity to all the devils. From there we ascended to the floor above. The most absolute darkness continued to reign on the staircase, and what a staircase! At our noise, there were prolonged grumblings from the two sleepers with not very reassuring faces. However, at the second floor, the bedroom door was closed and the policemen knocked, shouted, recited their names and ranks to obtain admittance, but the terrified tenants, fearing an ambush, at first refused point-blank. We remained thus for a moment one hanging from another, a trailing human vine in the stairwell. I stood still, able to see not an inch before me, and I seemed always to hear one of those two sleepers coming up behind me onto the landing where I was lingering, ready to impress upon me by force that I must not disturb the sleep of honest citizens. Finally the door on the second floor opened. Under siege from the police officers, the occupants of this chamber consented to grant us access. The constables brought all their lanterns out at once and shone their light onto the bed to bring it into view. We, excited by I know not what anxious curiosity, burst into the poor garret at the same moment. Dear God! What wretchedness! That there should be creatures so utterly abandoned! No glass in the windows, where hung, in place of drapes, a filthy piece of tartan which must serve to cover both shoulders and windows, a shawl by day and a curtain by night. A poor blanket on the bed, a meagre straw mattress and three young girls who had just been sleeping one crammed against another, three girls aged sixteen, pale and worn out by hunger and misery. How dreadful the winter must be for these unfortunates – and how, when the season of freezing fogs arrives, will they endure the cold at night and all the extremes of weather? Poor girls, who have perhaps been hungry since the day that they were born! I looked closely at their fair young heads, which had still preserved an air of innocence, and in the presence of such misery I involuntarily recalled these beautiful lines of the poet:

> Never insult a woman for her fall!
> Who knows what burdens her poor soul must bear?
> Who knows how long she has been hunger's thrall?*

Mr Price wanted to interrogate these poor little beggars in our presence. They showed their heads, which they until then had been trying to hide, not under the bedclothes, which were not long enough, but through their hands. Then, sitting up, they modestly covered their fronts with their arms and stared at us with extreme sweetness. A kind of naive astonishment could be read in their gaze, and we all found these three young faces deeply appealing.

"What are your names, young ladies?" asked the inspector with that discreet courtesy which the English show to women of all conditions.

"I'm Mary. My friends are Betsy and Jenny," answered one who was more self-assured than her companions.

"How old are you?"

"Sixteen and seventeen."

"Are your parents alive?"

"We never knew them."

"Why aren't you working?"

"We had work last month, but then they stopped it, for the end of the season. We haven't been able to find work anywhere else."

"So where did you work?"

"In a dressmaker's."

"And what do you do now?"

Here there fell a distressing silence. The poor little creatures begged, searched the heaps of refuse in the street for items to sell, or even for something to eat, and at night – for the modest sum of a penny, the three of them came to this disgusting garret to rest for a moment on a horrible pallet, at the mercy of villains, thieves and vagabonds of the worst sort. We sorrowfully withdrew, leaving some coins for these unhappy girls, who thanked us with tears in their eyes.

Inspector Price told me that these ruinous hovels where beggars come to lodge at night are "not under our supervision", and such is the English respect for the liberty of the individual that the police usually only enter them with circumspection. In these appalling garrets many things happen worthy of pity and compassion, and we were told of a poor devil who died of hunger amidst a heap of rags, where he had fallen asleep on the floor in one of these hideous dens where beggars and abandoned girls spend the night, and was half eaten by rats and dogs. The houses we had explored before these were certainly superior. Indeed, some semblance of order reigns in those; in authorizing them, the police reserve the right to inspect them, and the rules of hygiene are to some extent observed. There is good ventilation and fires are lit. The dormitories may only hold a fixed number of persons, the beds are numbered and distinct, the sexes are separated. But as for the attics and garrets reserved for the homeless, "the destitute and desolate", as the police call them, how dreadful it is to see them, and how sick at heart we felt as we left the garret where Mary and her companions spend such miserable nights!

It was three in the morning when we quitted the place. At the police station where Mr Price took us next was the jail where they held the drunken and disorderly who had been picked up on the public streets. Some of the cells were opened for us. One was crammed with men peacefully sleeping off their wine or bandaging their recent wounds. A few of them, recognizing Inspector Price through the fumes of Bacchus, tried to protest at their detention, but the door was promptly shut in their faces. Another cell contained women, less tranquil than the men and chattering frenziedly, for which the drink was their excuse. A third den held a horrible spectacle: a woman was alone there because she was in the throes of delirium tremens, her hair hanging wildly over her shoulders, her eyes crazed, her face bloodied by her own nails as she scraped them across it, the true image of a harpy. When she realized Mr Price had arrived, she called out, "Let me out, Inspector, I want to go, I want to go home.

The drunk woman in prison

My husband and children are expecting me!" The heart of a wife and mother was coming to life amid the drunkenness. "Open this door so I can go home!" Then, passing from rage to good humour, she said, "Come on, Mr Price my dear. Let me go, old friend. I promise I'll be good."

And then, seeing that no one was listening to her, she exclaimed, "It's a lie! I'm not drunk, it's a dirty trick by those coppers. I'm going to complain to a judge tomorrow..."

And she beat her head against the walls of the cell, rattled the door on its hinges, rolled on the floor, foaming at the mouth, uttering unintelligible words and shouting ceaselessly. We spent nearly half an hour there, and for all that half-hour the Fury never stopped shouting. Sometimes she called to us, and at others she called imaginary creatures to her aid. Twice I tried to meet her gaze through the spyhole of the door, and twice I recoiled almost in fear of this furious madwoman who was trying to throw herself at me in spite of the door blocking her way. A constable pulled back the flap for a moment, and then she became calm, asking in the gentlest of voices if she might be set free. "Yes, free tomorrow morning," the officer told her kindly, and the shrew fell silent.

The various spectacles, one after another, to which we had been witnesses during that night, so strangely spent, had left us singularly moved and almost stupefied. Four o'clock had just struck, and day was breaking in London, where at a latitude of fifty-two degrees the sun sets almost as late and rises almost as early as in St Petersburg. We were in need of air and light. Thanking the indulgent inspector and his officers, we hastened to leave those muddy districts in which we had just spent six long hours. London Bridge was not far off, and we walked there to seek a little cool and comfort from the bridge over the Thames.

The factory chimneys stretching between London, Southwark and Blackfriars Bridges on the right bank of the river were already beginning to send a smoky shadow into the air. The machine rooms, breweries and tanneries of this industrial quarter were resuming their daily labours, while on the left bank, downstream from the old tower which dominates that part of the city, the ships at anchor seemed to be rousing from their night-long sleep. Some boats were beginning to move, and here and there the sound of hammer on anvil and the strident whistle of a steamer could be heard. A light mist, detaching itself from the surface of the river, whose lazy waters make their way so slowly to the sea, rose onto both banks and obscured some of the city without ever quite hiding from view the imposing façade of the Palace of Westminster, which bathes its feet in the Thames, and the bold dome of St Paul's, the metropolitan cathedral of old London. What painter, what traveller, passing over the bridge where we stood, has not fixed his eyes for a moment on this unique view which Canaletto would have envied, for it has only Venice as an equal – and how well the charming tableau which was developing ever more clearly before our gaze with the ever more lively touch of dawn was suited to soothe our spirits from the sorrowful feelings of the night! But the tableau must have a stain upon it, and we might have wished to draw a veil over the foreground. On one of London Bridge's stone benches, two soldiers lying side by side, and next to them a young girl with her bonnet untied, were deeply asleep in spite of the morning's chill. This sight recalled us to the expedition we had just made. Despite the change of district, similar spectacles would occur all the way to our lodgings. On the Strand, the nocturnal orgy was continuing in defiance of morning, and when we got back to our rooms, the pubs of Haymarket, still open, still lit, were accommodating their eternal drinkers leaning on the marble-topped tables. A group of women who roamed this dreadful district between midnight and four in the morning had also remained in the cafés. In the street, hidden in doorways, little urchins were crammed one on top of another. Four policemen were solemnly carrying the dead body of a drunken woman along the street on a stretcher.

Such are the regrettable spectacles which unfold before the eyes of the curious at night in the poor parts of London. I have not exaggerated my portrayal: I have written only what I saw. Others before me, witnessing the same miseries, have spoken of them more eloquently. Who has not read what Léon Faucher,* one of the glories of French political economy, has written on this subject? Who does not know the arresting articles of Alphonse Esquiros,* who so nobly employed his long years of leisure in exile by studying England and English life? Both these masters must be read again and quoted here, because their moving and truthful accounts will confirm my own.

As Léon Faucher says in his *Studies of England*, "The Blackwall railway crosses the whole length of Whitechapel. Looking down from the viaduct which carries the tracks, the gaze plunges freely into the secrets of this wretchedness.

A trio of sleepers

Four policemen at work

One catches sight of gaunt women revealing themselves half naked at windows; pale children wallowing in the mud of the squares with the pigs that are the inseparable companions of Irish families; tattered cloths hanging above the streets as if designed to intercept the light as well as the warmth; here and there in the open spaces, piles of bricks and filth; and everywhere fetid pools which attest to the absence of any system of running water. This is the spectacle presented by Whitechapel from a bird's-eye view. How would it be if, by an act of imagination which on this occasion has nothing diabolical about it, one could lift off the roofs of the houses and count the groans and imprecations breathed from them to Heaven?"

And elsewhere, speaking of those foul districts of Spitalfields and Bethnal Green, swarming with 150,000 weavers, mostly Irish, the celebrated economist tells us that "the houses of this district are in a state of dilapidation of which it is quite impossible to convey an idea. They are often built of ill-fitting boards, which quickly gives them the appearance of the most disgusting cowsheds. When these hovels are condemned because of the danger which they pose to those who live there, and once the tenants have abandoned them, but before they have been knocked down, there will always be some Irish family there unable to pay for lodgings who come like foul animals seeking shelter. In a district where wet weather floods the streets, fever wastes no time in breathing forth from these pestilent ruins."

And later M. Léon Faucher says, "Transport a colony of Dutchmen into these districts, people who wash and scrub all day long, as enamoured of order and propriety as these strange denizens are of the base disorder which seems to be their element, and you would see nothing done ever again... We might almost say it was one of those medieval villages walled in by the magistrates for protection against an external enemy, but that they give themselves over, in the absence of upkeep, in their native ignorance, to the murderous action of epidemics. The last houses of the city hide the streets of Whitechapel like ramparts: one may only enter them by way of winding passages opened under the arches or between the damp walls of the courtyards. It is an entire city reserved for pedestrians. Since fever decimated the population, it was decided that cesspits should be dug in the principal streets – and what streets! But the removal of the refuse is only carried out once a week; for seven days it is heaped up in the public highway, which is thus covered in a permanent bed of manure."

One can see from these lines, chosen at random from *Studies of England*, that the picture of these poor districts has not been at all overstated. Léon Faucher is certainly a trustworthy witness, an economist before he became a literary author, and writing not for the pleasure of moving the reader with dramatic situations or even with sonorous phrases and finely modulated sentences.

Let us now move on to another observer, no less exact, no less conscientious, whose always truthful brush will paint us the inhabitants of these terrible slums, these strange, dark haunts.

In *England and English Life*, Esquiros says, "Whoever has attentively visited the populous districts typical of the city of London must have come across these words written by hand or printed on a notice: 'Good beds – abundant hot water – gas all night'. The house bearing this sign is not, truth to tell, distinguishable in any way from the other houses in the neighbourhood, except by a character of sadness and of dirt. Sometimes, however, one can identify them by another feature: the windows, almost on a level with the pavement, have more sheets of paper in them than glass. It is an acknowledged principle in the world of such establishments that windows are made not to admit light but to keep out cold air.

"...Accompanied by a policeman, I entered many of these establishments, and at different hours of the day and night. The most dreadful house that I visited is in Fox Court (Gray's Inn Lane), which is inhabited only by prostitutes and thieves. The first time I availed myself of the local policeman's services, we were forbidden to cross the threshold of this lodging house because the tenants were not yet up. It was eleven in the morning and there was a dense fog. My guide told me that this last circumstance, had it been known by the sleepers, would certainly have drawn them into the street, because it was a fine opportunity for them to practise their trade.

"...The lodgings for 'travellers' (a euphemism) are far from presenting a character of order and cleanliness. There are some in which noise, confusion and indescribable filth prevail; where the pale, rickety walls offer scant shelter to faces still paler than the walls themselves; where one stifles in summer and freezes in winter. One 'traveller' tells how, some years ago, he slept near Drury Lane in a room where the ceiling consisted of a slate roof which had been stripped bare by the wind and allowed such a clear view of the sky that he could count the stars.

"A great variety of persons frequent these establishments, but they are principally drawn from among the itinerant trades. Men are grouped in such establishments by virtue of this law of chemistry: *like attracts like*. Those whose manners and occupations exhibit similar qualities on the public highway by day live together under the same roof by night.

"The interior of these houses, with certain exceptions and in certain districts, does not exhibit the scenes of tumult which one might imagine would be occasioned by a gathering of individuals who make such a noise in the streets and at the crossroads. The predominant feature of this itinerant community is, on the contrary, silence. Some smoke, others sleep, others still prepare their supper. They all gather around the hearth, because what these men are seeking above all, having been exposed all day to the inclemency of the street, is warmth. I was struck by their extremely reserved expressions, but all the more astonished to find, in most of the boarding houses I visited, at least one newspaper.

"Most English moralists consider the numerous 'low' boarding houses as schools of vice and dens of iniquity, and with good reason. Some among them have even held that the existence of these houses is an insurmountable obstacle to the development and improvement of the poorer classes. The cramming of individuals into airless rooms, the mingling of the sexes – at least in the kitchens – the bad examples and bad teachings, undoubtedly exercise a pernicious influence on the health and morals of the 'travellers'. One finds young girls of fifteen and children separated from their families all jumbled together in these haunts of nocturnal cohabitation. To suppress these houses would be a measure incompatible with English notions on the right of property and individual liberty: it is not to be thought of. All that may be done is to challenge them with night-time refuges which the poor will find notably superior. British charity has already embarked on this course, but there are obstacles to be overcome, and one of these obstacles is that created by the chains of habit."

Let us see how the realist pen of Théophile Gautier, always such a close observer, depicts the rogues of Britain. "The people of London," says the illustrious author, "dress themselves at the second-hand store, and a gentleman's suit, descending from one degradation to another, finishes up on the back of a sewage worker, and the satin hat of a duchess on the vile neck of a servant girl. Even in St Giles, the wretched Irish quarter which exceeds in poverty all that one can imagine of horror and filth, one sees black hats and suits, worn most often with no shirt, and buttoned directly over the skin, which appears through the tears in the cloth."

Théophile Gautier goes on to say, "St Giles is two paces from Oxford Street and Piccadilly, and the contrast is not moderated by any gradual shading. You pass with no transition from the most flamboyant opulence to the most horrible misery. Carriages do not penetrate into these rutted and waterlogged alleyways where tattered children swarm, where older girls with their hair hanging loose, barefoot, barelegged, a meagre scrap of cloth scarcely covering their breasts, watch you with a crazed and ferocious stare. What suffering, what famine can be read upon these thin, haggard, begrimed and beaten faces, lashed by the cold! There are poor devils here who have been hungry every moment since they were weaned... From such privations the blood of those unfortunates deteriorates and turns from red to yellow, as the reports of physicians have noted."

One of the saddest aspects of the study of misery in London is the fact that it is everywhere. We visited it in its classic locations, those which have generally attracted the attention of moralists, economists and voyagers; but it exists elsewhere, and even the West End, the most aristocratic and elegant of districts in the new London, has its own sad and gloomy corners to show. As an English writer tells us: "In the superb district of Kensington, not far from the splendid royal gardens, there are entire streets of dreadful hovels planted in a soil slimy with refuse. One part of Kensington's wretched population lives in these noxious holes; another has taken refuge in gypsy caravans half-buried in the mud; and a third has nothing to live in but the detached carriage of a hackney cab, for which they pay a rent of six pence (sixty centimes) per week."

Quoting these lines in his *Guide to London*, M. Reclus* writes, "Still more unfortunate are those who have not even the carriage of a cab, and who must spend nights of fog or snow with no other recourse but to walk the streets or the broad lanes which enclose some of the parks. Even though there is no lack of furnished rooms in London where one may find a bed at two pence a night, there are sometimes thousands of people who have not enough money to pro-cure themselves even that vile refuge. Under the arches of Covent Garden, poor famished creatures spend all night walking and waiting anxiously for daybreak. Between four and five in the afternoon, during periods of misery that so often follow unemployment in various industries, one sees the unfortunates gather on the benches of the Mall and Birdcage Walk around St James's Park. Sometimes they have to push and shove to get a place, but at least it is better to sit on a wooden bench than to lie on the ground at the foot of a tree. At night the policeman, bound to follow orders, wakes the sleepers and warns them that it is prohibited to sleep on benches reserved for walkers. 'We aren't sleeping, we're walking,' reply the free citizens of England, and the policeman goes on his way. On Saturday and Sunday nights, sleepers are rarer on the benches of St James's and under the arches of Covent Garden. Then the wretches betake themselves to the 'gin palaces' in the hope of finding copper or silver coins dropped on the floor by drunkards."

To the authors from whom I have just borrowed so many extracts should be added Mayhew,* who is so popular in

Great Britain, and whose interesting and remarkable work *London Labour and the London Poor*, well known in France too, proclaims unstintingly to the rich metropolis the shames of its social plagues.

What palliatives can be applied to so many miseries? Is pauperism an irremediable vice, a plague which modern societies must accept without the hope of ever being released from it? Are great cities invariably fated to witness the sad spectacles of which London has just provided us an example? This is what I was asking myself on my return from the nocturnal excursion into Whitechapel, and it seems to me that, however little he may concern himself with the social movement and moral life of nations in our era, each of our readers should ask himself the same question. So then, what is the surest means of attaining the regeneration of the poor classes? I can see only one that is unanswerable: instruction, education! The English have done much in this direction, but still less than Switzerland and Germany. It is even the case that in Switzerland there are cantons where there are no poor people. Charitable institutions such as asylums, workhouses, rest homes for beggars and benevolent societies can only treat the illness. They do not stop it at its source; and besides, they do not benefit those shamefaced poor who are too timid to confront their wretchedness, to implore others openly to come to their aid. The temperance societies never correct more than the smallest proportion of drunkards; the Bible societies, the open-air preaching which is so much practised in London,* brings not a jot of religion to the degraded man who has lost the instinct for it. Some municipal ordinances merely increase the evil. To what purpose do you enjoin a day of rest if, as soon as the Sunday service is over, the taprooms and taverns, so briefly closed, are open again, and if the tap which pours beer from the counter never ceases to flow all day? The drinkers form a queue at the door, an occupation which brings benefit to another, and your police regulations serve only to augment the troubles in the street.

Therefore, to do battle efficaciously against pauperism and the train of vices which it brings behind it, education must at all costs be extended; it is still the best and most certain way of raising the moral and, at the same time, the intellectual level of the masses, and of giving them the habit of saving, the only one which can lead them towards well-being. In this connection, a curious trial was attempted in

London by the organization of street-sweepers and chimney sweeps. Some charitable persons enlisted poor abandoned orphans, gave them instruction and a trade instead of leaving them to roam the streets, wholly given over to their own devices. There is much reason to hope that one day they shall make good citizens; as we wait, they work, learn, earn themselves some savings, and each one is a victim snatched from certain misery, perhaps from the most abject vice. Education! Education! And with education, work: and pauperism shall disappear, and no one will say any longer that there are in London, at this hour, one hundred and twenty thousand individuals with neither hearth nor home – thieves, swindlers, pickpockets, tramps or beggars – and that every year in the Three Kingdoms there are more than ten thousand children under ten years of age convicted of criminal offences! What a haunt of bandits the United Kingdom would become, and what an unceasing threat its disinherited classes would pose to European society, if the colonies, Great Britain's immense waste pipe, did not exist! Irish emigration alone to the United States, Australia and India takes one hundred thousand paupers across the seas each year; but the colonies cannot suffice, for not everybody, not even those persons without a moral compass, will agree to his expatriation overseas. On the other hand, we have seen the limited efficacy of the other palliative measures in use against pauperism. The committees for welfare, savings and assistance remedy the evil less than inadequately. The ill must be cut off at the root; the pauper must be given an education from his tenderest infancy. Let schools spring up in the great city, free schools, Sunday schools, "ragged" schools, call them what you will, and, while teaching the children free of charge, provide evening classes also for the adults, both men and women, and you shall swiftly feel the beneficial effects of instruction so liberally, so broadly extended among the people! A great step has undoubtedly been taken, but there is a yet greater one to take, and the English, who never stop once they have set off on the high road, will not hesitate in reaching their destination.

I should add that a good method for raising the moral level of the disinherited classes is also to procure them innocent and morally instructive pastimes at the same price as those pernicious establishments which they frequent. Mayhew insists on this point. So, make the people moral by instructing and amusing them – but make them moral, or else this hideous social plague which we call pauperism, and which today extends its ravages ever further across modern states, will never disappear. England is perhaps subject to this evil more than any other nation, precisely because it is one of the most powerful. Let her show how to extirpate it; let her combat the monster; let her reach into the last haunts of misery, ignorance and vice; and all those evils which are such a national shame for her shall vanish, never to return.

Open-air preaching

Poor abandoned women

Note on the Text and Illustrations

This translation of *Memories of London* is based on the volume edition of 1874 (Milan: Fratelli Treves), which also contained an Italian translation of Louis Simonin's *An Excursion to the Poor Districts of London* – here translated from the 1862 French edition (Paris: L. Hachette et Cie). The illustrations provided in this edition are a selection of engravings from both of these volumes.

Notes

p. 4, *Fucini*: Renato Fucini (1843–1921), Italian novelist and poet.

p. 4, *Mais vous n'êtes pas malade*: "But you are not ill" (French).

p. 4, *like Hugo's Duchess Josiane… come to my arms*: From Book Three of Victor Hugo's *The Man Who Laughs* (1869).

p. 12, *Ghiberti's baptistery doors*: The most famous work of the Florentine artist Lorenzo Ghiberti (1378–1455).

p. 12, *The actor Garrick*: David Garrick (1717–79), one of the foremost English actors of the eighteenth century.

p. 21, *St James's Hospital*: An error by De Amicis: the hospital he is referring to is called St Thomas's.

p. 31, *the Battle of Abukir*: Abukir, in Egypt, was the site of Napoleon's important victory over the Ottomans in July 1799.

p. 32, *Mi paghi, no*: "You pay me, no!" (Italian).

p. 42, *I gasped... were death*: Dante, *Inferno* v, 141.

p. 42, *Pasquale Paoli*: Pasquale Paoli (1725–1807) was a Corsican patriot who died in exile in London.

p. 43, *Andrew Bell*: Andrew Bell (1753–1832) was a Scottish priest and educator.

p. 43, *the philanthropist... the steam engine*: Jonas Hanway (1712–86) was a celebrated traveller and philanthropist; Clifton Wintringham Jr (1720–94) was a distinguished physician; James Watt (1736–1819) was a mechanical engineer who helped improve the steam engine.

p. 44, *the stone on which Jacob... dreamt his visionary dream*: A reference to the Stone of Scone, a stone used in Scottish, then English and British coronations, which legend claims to be the stone which the Israelite patriarch

Jacob used as a pillow when he had his vision of God (Genesis 28:10–22).

p. 50, *Murillo's Madonnas*: Bartolomé Esteban Murillo (1617–82) was a Spanish Baroque painter who specialized in religious themes.

p. 51, *Pietri*: Probably a reference to the French politician Pierre Marie Pietri (1809–64).

p. 51, *Thiers*: Adolphe Thiers (1797–1877) was a French statesman and historian.

p. 51, *Prince Friedrich Karl... Jules Favre*: Prince Friedrich Karl of Prussia (1828–85) was a Prussian aristocrat and military officer who distinguished himself during the Franco-Prussian War. Jules Favre (1809–80) was a French statesman who negotiated the armistice and treaty with Bismarck following France's defeat in the Franco-Prussian War.

p. 53, *Youth is a time... great poet put it*: Another quotation from Book Three of Hugo's *The Man Who Laughs* (see third note to p. 4).

p. 64, *the leper in de Maistre's novel*: A reference to *The Leper from the City of Aosta* by Xavier de Maistre (1763–1852).

p. 77, *Monsieur D.B.*: The painter Jean-Baptiste Henri Durand-Brager (1814–79), whose engravings illustrated this essay.

p. 82, *Court of Miracles*: A term used in the nineteenth century to describe the slum districts of Paris.

p. 86, *Callot*: Jacques Callot (*c.*1592–1635) was a famous printmaker and draftsman, who depicted the diversity of life in early seventeenth-century France.

p. 92, *considering the price... in very good order*: It was in good order, but a night there was much more expensive than at the House of Chicken Feathers in Peking, which P. Huc tells us about in his *Chinese Empire*. There the poor who follow this famous and pioneering missionary pay only half a centime per night, and sleep warmly on down. "A large hall is filled along its entire length with one deep layer of chicken feathers. The beggars and vagabonds who have no home go to spend the night in this immense dormitory. Men, women, children, young and old – everyone is admitted. It is communism in the full force and meaning of the term. Each makes his own nest, lays himself and his belongings on this ocean of feathers and sleeps as best he can. When day breaks he must move on, and at the door an employee of the enterprise collects the agreed fee of one *sapek*. In deference no doubt to the principle of equality, there are no half-rates in the system, and children are obliged to pay as much as the adults.

"In this eminently philanthropic and moral foundation's earliest years, the administration of the house of chicken feathers provided each of its guests with a small blanket, but this detail of the arrangements was soon adjusted. The communards of the establishment having acquired the habit of taking away the blankets either for sale or as an additional piece of clothing during the extreme cold of winter, the management realized that they were on the way to complete and inevitable ruin. To remove the blanket entirely would have been too cruel and hardly proper. So it was necessary to seek a middle way in order to reconcile the interests of the establishment and the good conduct of the sleepers. Note how the solution to this social problem was achieved. An immense blanket was manufactured out of felt, so stupendously large as to cover the whole dormitory. By day it is hung from the ceiling like a gigantic canopy.

When everyone is lying down neatly among the feathers, it is lowered by means of numerous pulleys. It should be noted that care has been taken to make holes all over the blanket through which the sleepers may fit their heads, so as not to suffocate. As soon as day appears, the phalansteric blanket is hoisted; but only after the precaution has been taken of sounding a signal by a blow on a gong to wake the deepest sleepers and invite them to hide their heads in the feathers, so as not be seized round the neck by this collar and lifted into the air with the blanket. Then one sees the immense brood of beggars grovel and flounder in this repellent sea of down, hastily put on their wretched rags, and finally spread abroad in gangs throughout the city to seek, more or less lawfully, the means to live." (Huc, *The Chinese Empire*, Gaume Frères, 1862).

The same fact is recounted by Mme Bourboulon in her *Voyage to China*. See 'The House of Chicken Feathers' in *Around the World*, Year 5, 1865. (AUTHOR'S NOTE)

p. 95, *On leaving the taproom... Les Fèves*: In the matter of poor districts, there is no comparison between London and Paris. The gloomy nooks and crannies of la Cité, today happily vanished, the saddest passageways of Mouffetard, Saint-Victor and Saint-Marcel do not provoke the disgust nor hide so many miseries and vices as do the parts of London of which we speak. If we seek a reason for this, we must find it in the different characters of the two peoples, the diversity of their customs and laws, and finally the fact that Paris is much less populated than London, not being, as that city is, the metropolitan port of the entire world. However it may be, let us give thanks to Providence that the palm which so often falls to England in matters of economy and policy, may on this occasion be ours, and without dispute. (AUTHOR'S NOTE)

p. 103, *Never insult... hunger's thrall*: The opening lines of the untitled fourteenth poem in the 1836 collection *Songs of the Half-Light* by Victor Hugo.

p. 111, *Léon Faucher*: Léon Faucher (1803–54) was a French politician and economist, whose *Studies of England* was published in two volumes in 1845.

p. 111, *Alphonse Esquiros*: Alphonse Esquiros (1812–1876) was a French novelist, poet, politician and essayist, who published several works on England in the 1860s, including *England and English Life* (1865).

p. 120, *Guide to London, M. Reclus*: Élisée Reclus (1830–1905) was a geographer and anarchist whose *Traveller's Guide to London and Its Surroundings* was published in 1860.

p. 121, *Mayhew*: The reformist social scientist and journalist Henry Mayhew (1812–87) wrote some influential articles on London's poor, compiled in the 1851 volume *London Labour and the London Poor*.

p. 123, *the open-air preaching... practised in London*: Open-air preaching is one of the spectacles which most astonish the foreigner on his arrival in London. Every evening, and often during the day on Sundays, along the promenades and in the busiest squares, men with austere faces and their heads bare, dressed in black with white cravats, a Bible under their arms, set themselves to read and preach. At first one passer-by will stop to listen, then two, and then a crowd gathers, carriages stop, men and women, soldiers and civilians, the old and the young gravely surround the preacher. In the slow, quiet, modulated voice that many Protestant ministers use when preaching or expounding the Bible, he pours forth his harangue; and not a word, not one mocking cry escapes from the audience. This unfailing calm is one of the distinctive traits of the English nation. In Paris, if the police were to permit open-air preaching in the first place, it would be no more than two minutes before the heckling, the jibes and even projectiles would start to fly, and not only from the ragamuffins. (AUTHOR'S NOTE)

ALMA CLASSICS

ALMA CLASSICS aims to publish mainstream and lesser-known European classics in an innovative and striking way, while employing the highest editorial and production standards. By way of a unique approach the range offers much more, both visually and textually, than readers have come to expect from contemporary classics publishing.

∽

To order any of our titles and for up-to-date information about our current and forthcoming publications, please visit our website on:

www.almaclassics.com